SOUPS
FOR YOUR
SLOW COOKER

Other cookery books by Spring Hill, an imprint of How To Books

THE EVERYDAY HALOGEN OVEN COOKBOOK
Quick, easy and nutritious recipes for all the family

SLOW COOK, FAST FOOD
Over 250 healthy, wholesome slow cooker and one pot meals for all the family

PERFECT BAKING WITH YOUR HALOGEN OVEN
How to create tasty bread, cupcakes, bakes, biscuits and savouries

THE EVERYDAY HALOGEN FAMILY COOKBOOK
Another 200 delicious meals and treats from the author of The Everyday Halogen Oven Cookbook

EAT WELL, SPEND LESS
The complete guide to everyday family cooking

HALOGEN COOKING FOR TWO

THE HEALTHY LIVING DIET COOKBOOK

For advice about everyday cooking visit www.everydaycookery.com

Write or phone for a catalogue to:

How To Books
Spring Hill House
Spring Hill Road
Begbroke
Oxford
OX5 1RX
Tel: 01865 375794

Or email: info@howtobooks.co.uk

Visit our website www.howtobooks.co.uk to find out more about us and our books.

Like our Facebook page **How To Books & Spring Hill**

Follow us on **Twitter@Howtobooksltd**

Read our books online www.howto.co.uk

SOUPS
FOR YOUR
SLOW COOKER

How to make delicious soups
for all occasions in your slow cooker

DIANA PEACOCK

SPRING HILL

Published by Spring Hill, an imprint of How To Books Ltd
Spring Hill House, Spring Hill Road
Begbroke, Oxford OX5 1RX
United Kingdom
Tel: (01865) 375794
Fax: (01865) 379162
info@howtobooks.co.uk
www.howtobooks.co.uk

First published 2012

How To Books greatly reduce the carbon footprint of their books
by sourcing their typesetting and printing in the UK.

British Library Cataloguing in Publication Data
A catalogue record of this book is available from the British Library.

ISBN: 978 1 905862 20 7

Illustrations by Firecatcher Creative
Produced for How To Books by Deer Park Productions, Tavistock,
Devon
Typeset by TW Typesetting, Plymouth, Devon
Printed and bound in Great Britain by Bell & Bain Ltd, Glasgow

NOTE: The material contained in this book is set out in good faith
for general guidance and no liability can be accepted for loss or
expense incurred as a result of relying in particular circumstances on
statements made in the book. Laws and regulations are complex and
liable to change, and readers should check the current position with
relevant authorities before making personal arrangements.

Contents

Introduction

When my husband Paul and I got married we were given a slow cooker as a wedding present. I used it a couple of times but was so concerned about the do's and don'ts that I never really used it properly. Although there is in fact nothing to worry about in terms of safely leaving your slow cooker on, we never wanted to leave it cooking while we were at work. I gave it away to a friend who used it correctly for years. We bought ourselves a new one a few years ago – the instructions were simple and we have never looked back. After about 10–15 minutes preparation time, you can leave the meal to cook by itself.

Slow cookers can be purchased quite cheaply from most supermarkets, and the supermarket own brand ones are generally very good quality. They are also very straightforward to use. The simpler basic models, which are excellent to make soups with, are probably all you need.

Slow cooking is an easy and versatile way of cooking, allowing you to make hearty meals without worrying. Soups are very popular in our household and they can be made in your slow cooker simply and successfully.

After years of making soup on the hob, I have found that slow cooking gives soup a fuller, richer depth of flavour. The ingredients blend together gently as they cook to produce a delightful and satisfying end result, suitable for any occasion.

Conversion Charts

This book provides metric measurements, but those who prefer Imperial, or who want to use US measures, can use these conversions.

WEIGHT	
Metric	*Imperial*
25g	1oz
50g	2oz
75g	3oz
100g	4oz
150g	5oz
175g	6oz
200g	7oz
225g	8oz
250g	9oz
300g	10oz
350g	12oz
400g	14oz
450g	1lb

OVEN TEMPERATURES	
Celsius	*Fahrenheit*
110°C	225°F
120°C	250°F
140°C	275°F
150°C	300°F
160°C	325°F
180°C	350°F
190°C	375°F
200°C	400°F
220°C	425°F
230°C	450°F
240°C	475°F

LIQUIDS		
Metric	*Imperial*	*US cup*
5ml	1 tsp	1 tsp
15ml	1 tbsp	1 tbsp
50ml	2fl oz	3 tbsp
60ml	$2\frac{1}{2}$fl oz	$\frac{1}{4}$ cup
75ml	3fl oz	$\frac{1}{3}$ cup
100ml	4fl oz	scant $\frac{1}{2}$ cup
125ml	$4\frac{1}{2}$fl oz	$\frac{1}{2}$ cup
150ml	5fl oz	$\frac{2}{3}$ cup
200ml	7fl oz	scant 1 cup
250ml	10fl oz	1 cup
300ml	$\frac{1}{2}$pt	$1\frac{1}{4}$ cups
350ml	12fl oz	$1\frac{1}{3}$ cups
400ml	$\frac{3}{4}$pt	$1\frac{3}{4}$ cups
500ml		2 cups
600ml	1pt	$2\frac{1}{2}$ cups

MEASUREMENTS	
Metric	*Imperial*
5cm	2in
10cm	4in
13cm	5in
15cm	6in
18cm	7in
20cm	8in
25cm	10in
30cm	12in

Store Cupboard Stashes for Your Soup

A well-stocked store cupboard is useful for all cooking and making soup is no different. You will always be able to make what you fancy at a moment's notice.

I grow some fresh herbs in the garden and during the winter months I grow parsley, thyme and chives inside on the kitchen windowsill. This means I always have some fresh green colour to add to the soup if necessary.

Good stock gives a soup an excellent start, so make your own or buy stock cubes that are of a high quality. Organic cubes do not necessarily mean the best flavour so try several brands of stock cube, powder or paste to see which makes a difference to the soup's finished flavour.

A good tip is to buy a little extra meat and freeze it, ready for when you wish to make a soup. As soups make meat go further than any other recipe, having 200–400g batches of beef, chicken, pork and lamb in the freezer is always a good idea. It means you will have a good meal even when the purse is empty. I also buy 2–3 ham or pork hocks and freeze them for when I need them.

The spice rack
Black peppercorns
Cayenne pepper
Chilli flakes
Chinese five-spice powder
Coriander, ground
Cumin, ground
Curry powder, mild and medium
Paprika
Turmeric

Dried herbs
Basil
Bay leaves
Mixed herbs
Oregano
Parsley
Rosemary
Sage
Tarragon
Thyme

Dried ingredients

Beans, borlotti or cannellini
Country soup mix, a mixture of beans, barley and lentils – this is a
    definite store cupboard ingredient
Lentils, red and green
Marrowfat peas
Pearl barley
Rice, long-grain white and brown

The tinned and packeted department

Beans – if you prefer to buy ready-to-use beans, stock a few different
    types such as butter beans, red kidney and cannellini
Garlic purée, in a tube
Noodles, dried
Passata
Pasta shapes
Suet for making dumplings
Tomato purée, in a tube
Tomatoes, chopped

The freezer

So long as frozen ingredients are defrosted before you use them, they will
make slow cooking soup even easier.

Broccoli
Cauliflower
Green beans
Peas
Peppers – for ease and speed, I have started to buy ready-chopped
    frozen peppers and onions
Onions
Sweetcorn

CHAPTER 1

Hints and Tips

The most important tip is to read the manufacturer's instructions as slow cookers vary quite a lot. Practise making simple dishes so you get to know your cooker and don't leave it for too long at the beginning until you know how long it takes to cook things. My cooker is a basic model with high, low and warm settings. I use the high setting the most as it obviously cooks more quickly. But the low setting is useful if you need to go out, as it takes much longer to cook. Using the low setting usually takes about double the time as cooking on high, but this is very approximate and you need to get to know your cooker.

A slow cooker generally works by heating the ingredients from an element in the outer container from the base and slightly up the sides, so always be careful when touching the appliance as the outer container does get very hot.

The great thing is you can start cooking on high and then turn to the low setting before you go out. Slow cooking is particularly good in the summer months when you want a hot meal but the thought of heating the conventional oven is just too daunting. The slow cooker doesn't overpower you with heat like an ordinary cooker.

Reasons for using a slow cooker

Slow cookers are much more energy efficient than a conventional oven in that they use approximately

200–250 watts – a conventional oven uses about 700 watts.

Slow cookers are ideal for making soups, and stews and casseroles for that matter, because the long, slow cooking allows flavours to develop and is great for tenderising tougher, cheaper cuts of meat.

However, one of the greatest benefits of using a slow cooker is that it allows you to prepare a dish well in advance so that you can come home, even if you've been out all day at work, to a welcoming hot meal.

Buying a slow cooker

Slow cookers come in various sizes, from 1.5 litres, which is ideal for a couple, up to 6.5 litres, which is more suitable for a large family or for entertaining. It's worth noting that you can't fill a slow cooker to the rim, so if you are using a 5-litre cooker, for example, it will in fact only produce about 4 litres of food.

Slow cookers range in price from £20 to over £100, but you can certainly get a very good and reliable appliance in the £20–35 price range.

A glass lid is a good idea because you can keep an eye on what's going on inside without lifting the lid and losing precious heat.

Pre-heating your slow cooker

Make sure the slow cooker is either at room temperature or ideally pre-heated before adding ingredients as this speeds up the cooking time. Most appliances can be pre-heated while you prepare the ingredients.

I usually use my slow cooker to 'sweat' some of the ingredients as it pre-heats, giving the soup a better flavour. For example, I use it to sweat the vegetables for about 20 minutes whilst it is preheating. If you prefer to speed up this process, cook the ingredients in a large frying pan for 3–4 minutes instead. So if the following recipes ask you to add certain ingredients to the slow cooker whilst it is heating up, remember that you can cook them in the frying pan instead if you prefer.

Getting the best out of your slow cooker

I tend not to cook ingredients in other pans to speed up the cooking time – I only do this when it adds to the flavour of a recipe. I have found the flavour of the finished soup is superior if it is all done in the cooker. However, I do like to pre-cook the meat in a separate pan, even if I am using minced meat, as the finished flavour is better and you know it has reached a high temperature prior to slow cooking.

Cans of vegetables or cartons of ingredients like passata are easily heated in a bowl in the microwave prior to adding to the cooker pot. Stock is best added at either boiling or as close to boiling as possible and is usually added after all the other ingredients – this gets the cooking process going more rapidly.

Always defrost any vegetables before adding to the pot. It is very tempting just to throw a handful of frozen peas or beans into the soup as it cooks, but this can add as much as an extra hour to the cooking time.

Don't be tempted to keep stirring the ingredients, as every time you remove the lid the cooking temperature goes down. Stir everything well when you add ingredients and then leave it for at least 1 ½ hours before stirring again if you have to.

I don't add any thickening agents such as flour or cornflour to my soups, as I prefer them as they are and many are in fact thickened by the other ingredients.

Important things to remember

- Read the manufacturer's instructions before using your appliance.

- Appliances vary, so practice with simple recipes before leaving the house for long periods whilst it is cooking. The cooking times given in the recipes are very approximate and will vary depending on the age and make of your appliance.

- Always thaw frozen foods before adding to the pot.

- When using dried peas or beans, soak and pre-boil them following the packet's instructions. This is particularly important when using red kidney beans, as they are toxic if not boiled for a certain length of time.

- Slow cooking has a tendency to reduce the colour of green vegetables and can spoil the fresh look of a dish, although it never impairs the flavour. You can compensate for this by adding fresh herbs prior to serving.

- Always take care as the appliance gets very hot.

- If you are using butter instead of oil at the beginning of the recipe, spread it over the base of the slow cooker as though you were greasing a dish. This ensures the butter melts quickly as the cooker heats up.

Accompaniments

Some recipes include serving suggestions, as the accompaniments are often the favourite part of the dish in our household. Other recipes don't include accompaniments, as I tend to vary what we have with these soups. Some soups stand on their own, such as the noodle or pasta-based ones. I am sure you will find your own favourite accompaniments to the recipes!

Serving number

All of the recipes in this book serve 4–6 people, generously.

CHAPTER 2

Vegetable Soups

Using your slow cooker to make vegetable soups seems to add another dimension to their flavour. They are richer and have more depth in comparison to soups made on the hob. This is down to the length of time the ingredients are cooked together for – the flavours are gently blended to produce an amazing soup, for which you would pay pounds for just a small serving in a restaurant. Slow-cooked soups are still, however, nutritious and satisfying. Even the simplest of ingredients turns into something very special, as you will find out for yourself when you make the first recipe in the following vegetable collection.

Simple Vegetable

Ingredients:
15g butter or 2 tbsp vegetable oil
1 onion, finely chopped
1 large carrot, finely diced
1 stick celery, finely chopped
1 red pepper, chopped
1 green or yellow pepper, chopped
1.3 litres vegetable or chicken stock,
    or just water, heated until hot
Salt and black pepper to taste
100g whole green beans, chopped
    into 2cm pieces
100g fresh or frozen peas, defrosted
1 tbsp chopped chives
2-3 sage leaves, chopped
1 tbsp freshly chopped parsley

No fuss, just wonderful flavour. I often put all the vegetables, except for the beans and peas, into my food processor and let it chop them for me.

1. Heat the slow cooker on high, adding the butter or oil, whilst you prepare the ingredients.

2. After the cooker has heated for about 10 minutes, add the onion, carrot and celery. Stir and leave for 10 minutes.

3. Add the peppers, stir in the hot stock or water, season and stir well.

4. Add the beans and peas and stir again. Put on the lid and leave for about 4 hours on high or for 6 ½ hours on low.

5. Stir in the herbs, cover and cook for 30 more minutes or 1 hour if cooking on low.

6

Tomato and Lentil

Tomatoes and lentils are a wonderful combination in this soup.

1. Heat the slow cooker on high, adding the butter or oil, whilst you prepare the ingredients.

2. Add the onion, carrot, celery, tomatoes, garlic and tomato purée. Stir, cover and cook for 15 minutes.

3. Combine the stock and passata in a saucepan or bowl and either heat on the hob or in the microwave until very hot but not boiling.

4. Stir the stock mixture into the ingredients in the cooker and add the lentils, sundried tomatoes, oregano and seasoning. Stir everything well. Cover and cook on high for 4 hours or on low for 7 hours.

5. Just before serving, stir in the basil leaves.

Ingredients:
15g butter or 2 tbsp vegetable oil
1 onion, chopped
1 medium-sized carrot, finely chopped
1 stick celery, chopped
4 large or 6 smaller ripe tomatoes, thinly sliced
1 clove garlic, chopped
2 rounded tbsp tomato purée
700ml vegetable or chicken stock
500ml passata
80g red lentils
5 sundried tomatoes in oil, chopped
½ tsp dried oregano
Salt and black pepper to taste
Small handful fresh basil leaves, optional (or parsley or dill if you prefer)

Light Summer Vegetable

Ingredients:
2 tbsp olive, sunflower or rapeseed oil
1 medium-sized onion or 5 small shallots, finely chopped
2 sticks celery, finely chopped
2 small young carrots, finely chopped
1 red pepper, chopped
1 green pepper, chopped
Pinch salt
1.2 litres vegetable or chicken stock, heated until hot
Salt and pepper to taste
1 heaped tbsp chopped chives
1 heaped tbsp chopped parsley

The slow cooker is ideal for use during the summer months, as the kitchen doesn't ever get overpoweringly hot as it can do if you use the hob or oven. This soup is great when you want something warming yet light.

1. Heat the slow cooker on high, adding the oil of your choice, whilst you prepare the vegetables.

2. Add the vegetables and salt and stir well. Cover and leave to cook for 20 minutes on high.

3. Add the hot stock, stir then cover and leave for 4 hours on high or 6 ½ hours on low.

4. Stir in the herbs and cook for 30 more minutes on high or 1 hour on low.

● **Vegetable Soups**

Mediterranean Vegetable and Olive

A delicious taste of the Med, especially when served with some garlic and herb focaccia.

1. Heat the slow cooker on high whilst you prepare the courgette and aubergine.

2. Heat 2 tbsp oil in a large frying pan and fry the courgette and aubergine quickly until slightly brown all over.

3. Whilst the vegetables are frying, add another 2 tbsp oil to the cooker and stir in the onion, garlic, peppers and oregano.

4. Add the courgette and aubergine mixture and stir in the can of tomatoes and the hot stock.

5. Stir well and cover with the lid. Cook on high for 4½ hours or 7 hours on low.

6. Stir in the olives and add the salt and pepper to taste. Cook for 30 more minutes on high or 1 hour on low.

7. Add the basil prior to serving.

Ingredients:
2 courgettes, chopped
1 small aubergine or ½ large, cut into small cubes
4 tbsp olive oil
1 onion, finely chopped
2 cloves garlic, chopped
1 red pepper, chopped
1 yellow pepper, chopped
1 level tsp dried oregano
1 × 400g can chopped tomatoes
700ml stock, heated until hot
12-15 pitted black olives, chopped
Salt and pepper to taste
Small handful basil leaves

Leek and Potato

Ingredients:
15g butter
1 small onion, finely chopped
2 large leeks, chopped into fairly
  small pieces
3 large potatoes, peeled and cut into
  small chunks
½ tsp dried sage
Salt and white or black pepper to
  taste
1.3 litres stock or water, heated until
  hot
100ml single cream
1 tbsp freshly chopped parsley

Leeks and potatoes are amazing ingredients for a soup as they combine to make a wonderfully savoury blend. I like to serve this with some crispy toast.

1. Heat the slow cooker on high, adding the butter, whilst you prepare the vegetables.

2. Add all the other ingredients except the stock, cream and parsley. Stir everything well and put on the lid. Leave for 20 minutes.

3. Add the stock and stir again. Cover and leave to cook for 5 hours on high or 7 ½ hours on low.

4. Stir in the cream and parsley. Cover and leave for 30 minutes.

Vegetable Soups

Root Vegetable

This is one for the frosty days of winter or any cold day.

1. Preheat the oven to 220°C/Gas Mark 7 and prepare the vegetables.

2. Place the vegetables in a roasting tin and drizzle with the oil. Coat all the vegetables with the oil using your hands. Season with salt and pepper and place in the oven to roast for about 25 minutes or until they become slightly golden.

3. Heat the slow cooker on high and then add the semi-roasted vegetables.

4. Stir in the onion, garlic and dried herbs, then cover and cook for 10 minutes.

5. Stir in the stock and cover. Leave to cook for 5 hours on high or 7½ hours on low.

6. Add the chives about 30 minutes before serving.

Ingredients:
2 medium-sized carrots, chopped into small chunks
2 parsnips, peeled and cut into small chunks
¼ swede, peeled and cut into small chunks
2 small turnips, peeled and cut into chunks
100g celeriac, peeled and cut into small chunks
3–4 tbsp vegetable oil
Salt and pepper to taste
1 onion, finely chopped
2 cloves garlic, chopped
½ tsp dried thyme
½ tsp dried rosemary
1.5 litres stock or water, heated until hot
1–2 tbsp chopped fresh chives

Split Pea

Ingredients:
15g butter or 2 tbsp vegetable oil
1 medium onion, finely chopped
1 clove garlic, chopped
3 sticks celery, chopped
3 medium carrots, diced
300g split peas
½ tsp dried thyme or 1 tsp fresh
    thyme leaves
½ tsp dried marjoram
1½ litres vegetable or trotter stock,
    heated until hot

This soup can be made using a stock made from 2 pigs' trotters, adding the meat just before the cooking time is finished. Simply cover the trotters in warm, lightly salted water, bring to the boil on the hob and then turn the heat down to a simmer. Cover and cook for 2 hours. Alternatively, keep the soup totally vegetarian if you prefer.

1. Heat the slow cooker on high, adding the butter or oil.

2. Add the onion, garlic, celery and carrots. Stir well and cover.

3. Wash the split peas well in cold water and then pour boiling water over them. Drain and add to the cooker.

4. Stir in the herbs and pour in the stock. Stir well, then cover and cook for 5 hours on high or 7 ½ hours on low.

Curried Pumpkin

An autumn favourite, made easy in the slow cooker.

Ingredients:
15g butter or 4 tbsp vegetable oil
1 onion, finely chopped
1 carrot, finely chopped
1 stick celery, chopped
1 level tbsp mild curry powder
½ tsp ground cinnamon
½ tsp ground cumin
½ tsp dried chilli flakes
2 cloves garlic, chopped
1 medium pumpkin, peeled, de-seeded and cut into 2cm chunks
1.2 litres stock, heated until hot
Salt and pepper to taste
1-2 tbsp freshly chopped coriander leaves

1. Heat the cooker on high, adding the butter or 2 tbsp oil. Add the onion, carrot, celery, curry powder, cinnamon, cumin, chilli and garlic. Stir and cover for about 20 minutes whilst you prepare the pumpkin.

2. Heat 2 tbsp oil in a frying pan and fry the pumpkin flesh until it just begins to brown.

3. Add the pumpkin to the cooker, stir in the stock and season with salt and pepper to taste. Cover and cook on high for 4–4 ½ hours or for 7 hours on low.

4. Stir in the coriander leaves just before serving.

Variation
Try adding 3 tbsp crème fraîche 30 minutes before the cooking time has finished.

Winter Vegetable and Barley

Ingredients:
15g butter
1 medium-sized onion, finely chopped
2 large carrots, chopped
2 sticks celery, chopped
1 large parsnip or 2 small, chopped
100g swede flesh, chopped
2 medium-sized potatoes, diced
80g pearl barley
1½ litres vegetable stock, heated until hot
1 tsp mustard powder or ready-made English mustard
½ tsp dried sage
½ tsp dried thyme
1 tsp dried parsley
Salt and pepper to taste
100g frozen peas, defrosted

Barley is so good for you and I often add it to soups and stews. It goes so well in this thick, winter-weight soup.

1. Heat the cooker on high, adding the butter.

2. Add all the vegetables (apart from the peas) and the barley, stirring them into the melted butter. Cover and leave for 20 minutes.

3. Stir in the stock, mustard and herbs. Season to taste with salt and pepper.

4. Cover and leave to cook for 3 hours. Then lift off the lid and stir in the defrosted peas. Leave to cook for another 2–2½ hours. Alternatively, cook on low for 6 hours, then add the peas and cook on high for 2 hours.

● Vegetable Soups

Ribollito

This is a Tuscan-style, farmhouse vegetable soup, thickened with bread. Use good quality white bread rather than wholemeal, as the flavour is better. Wholemeal bread can give a slightly bitter flavour to the soup.

Ingredients:
2 tbsp olive oil
1 onion, chopped
3 cloves garlic, chopped
1 leek, chopped
2 carrots, chopped
2 sticks celery, chopped
2 courgettes, sliced
2 waxy type potatoes, cubed
1 × 400g can chopped tomatoes
1 × 400g cannellini beans
½ tsp dried thyme
12 tsp dried oregano
1.2 litres vegetable, ham or chicken stock, heated until hot
½ Savoy cabbage or equivalent of curly kale
Salt and pepper to taste
4 thick slices white bread, at least a day old
Grana Padano cheese to serve

1. Heat the cooker on high and add the olive oil, onion, garlic and all the other vegetables except for the cabbage or kale, tomatoes and beans. Cover and cook for 25 minutes.

2. Stir in the tomatoes, beans and herbs.

3. Add the stock and cabbage or kale, then season with salt and pepper to taste.

4. Stir everything well, then add the slices of bread in large pieces. Cover and cook on high for 4½–5 hours or 7½–8 hours on low.

5. Thirty minutes before the cooking time is finished, stir the soup quickly to incorporate the bread.

6. Serve with lots of freshly grated Grana Padano cheese.

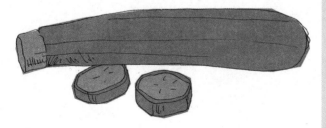

Beetroot

A Russian-style soup, that tastes sweet and is good with crispy croutons.

Ingredients:
15g butter
1 large onion, chopped
Approx. 750g beetroot, peeled and
    cut into 2cm chunks
2 medium-sized carrots, diced
2 medium-sized potatoes, peeled and
    cut into small pieces
½ small Savoy-type cabbage, finely
    shredded
3 tbsp tomato purée
1.2 litres stock, heated until hot
100ml red wine
2 bay leaves
Salt and pepper to taste
Sour cream to serve

1. Heat the slow cooker on high and add the butter.

2. Add the onion, beetroot, carrots and potatoes and stir well. Cover and cook for 20 minutes.

3. Add the cabbage and tomato purée and pour over the stock.

4. Add the red wine and bay leaves. Season with salt and pepper and stir everything well. Cover and cook for 4½–5 hours on high or 7½–8 hours on low.

5. Just before serving, swirl in 1 tbsp sour cream into each bowl of soup.

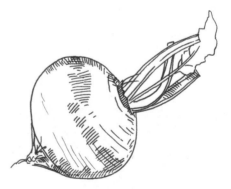

Thick Pea

Almost a stew, this soup is very filling and always reminds me of foggy days when I was young – mum would make it when the weather turned nasty. There's another meaty version of this soup in Chapter 5, using a ham hock.

Ingredients:
10g butter or 1 tbsp vegetable oil
1 large onion, finely chopped
1 large carrot, chopped. (This may be omitted but it adds a touch of sweetness to the soup.)
300g dried marrowfat peas, soaked overnight in cold water
2 bay leaves
½ tsp dried thyme or 2 stems fresh leaves
1.2 litres stock, heated until hot
Salt and pepper to taste

1. Heat the slow cooker on high and add the oil or butter and the onion and carrot.

2. Drain the peas and add to the cooker.

3. Add the bay leaves and thyme and stir in the stock.

4. Season to taste with salt and pepper and cover. Cook for 6 hours on high or 10 hours on low.

5. Add a little more stock if it is getting too thick for your taste after three-quarters of the cooking time.

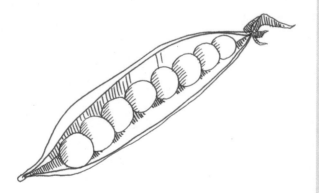

Mushroom

Ingredients:
25g butter
1 small onion, finely chopped
1 clove garlic, chopped
600g mushrooms
Juice of 1 lemon
1 level tsp paprika
1.2 litres stock, heated until hot
100ml dry white wine
Salt and pepper to taste
150ml single cream
2 tbsp freshly chopped parsley

This is a speedy soup to make, even in the slow cooker. It is a good one for a dinner party as you can prepare it a few hours ahead and it will cook itself whilst you prepare the other courses. Use any kind of mushrooms you like – a mixture is good for flavour.

1. Heat the slow cooker on high and add the butter, onion and garlic.

2. Chop the mushrooms into small pieces rather than slicing as they cook quicker. Stir them into the cooker.

3. Add the lemon juice, paprika, stock, wine and season to taste. Stir well and cover. Cook for 3 hours on high or 5 hours on low.

4. About 30 minutes before the cooking time is up, stir in the cream and parsley. More cream may be added if you wish, but I find this amount gives the best flavour.

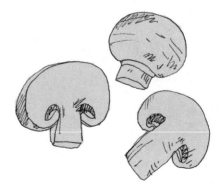

● **Vegetable Soups**

Three Bean

You can either use dried or canned beans for this soup – both give good results. I like to serve this with some crispy garlic and herb croutons.

1. Heat the slow cooker on high and add the butter or oil.

2. Add the onion, garlic, pepper, carrots and celery. Cover and cook for 20 minutes.

3. Drain the beans and add to the cooker.

4. Add the chilli or dried flakes and coriander and stir in the stock.

5. Season to taste with salt and pepper and cover and cook for 4½–5 hours on high or 8 hours on low.

6. Just before serving, stir in the freshly chopped coriander leaves.

Ingredients:
If using dried:
50g each borlotti and cannelloni beans, soaked overnight and rinsed in fresh water

Or:
1 × 400g can borlotti beans
1 × 400g can cannelloni beans
1 × 400g can red kidney beans (I always use canned, as dried kidney beans have to be boiled after soaking because of toxins.)
15g butter or vegetable oil
1 onion, finely chopped
1 clove garlic
1 red pepper, chopped
2 carrots, chopped
2 sticks celery, chopped
1 red chilli, chopped, or ½ tsp dried chilli flakes
½ tsp ground coriander
1.5 litres stock, heated until hot
Salt and pepper to taste
1-2 tbsp freshly chopped coriander leaves

Chargrilled Red Pepper and Tomato

Ingredients:
3 tbsp olive oil
1 onion, chopped
1 clove garlic, chopped
3 large red peppers
6 large, ripe tomatoes
Salt
1 tsp paprika
1.2 litres stock, heated until hot
2 bay leaves
Salt and pepper to taste
1 tbsp balsamic vinegar

This delicious soup is another quick cooker. It is scrumptious served with good crusty bread and butter and a sprinkle of your favourite cheese.

1. Preheat the grill if necessary and heat the slow cooker on high.

2. Add 1 tbsp oil to the cooker with the onion and garlic, stir and cover.

3. Cut the peppers in half, remove the seeds and place them skin-side up on a lightly oiled roasting tray. Quarter or halve the tomatoes and place them with the peppers, again skin-side up. Drizzle with the rest of the oil and season with a little salt. Grill for a few minutes until the skin chars.

4. Chop the peppers and tomatoes and place in the slow cooker.

5. Add the paprika, stock, bay leaves, salt and pepper and balsamic vinegar.

6. Stir well and cover. Cook for 3 hours on high or 5½–6 hours on low.

● **Vegetable Soups**

Thick Farmhouse Vegetable

I don't really know what 'farmhouse' means, but when I was little my mum used to buy a tin of thick, farmhouse vegetable soup. It was thick and glutinous due to the amount of barley in the recipe, and I loved it. But this homemade soup is far tastier.

1. Heat the cooker on high and add the butter or oil and the onion. Cover and leave for 15 minutes.

2. Drain the peas and lentils and the can of butter beans. Stir these and the other ingredients except for the parsley into the slow cooker.

3. Stir everything well and cover. Cook on high for 5½ hours or on low for 8 hours. Add a little more stock if the soup is getting too thick.

4. Just before serving stir in the parsley.

Ingredients:
50g each of yellow and green split peas and red lentils, soaked overnight
15g butter or 1 tbsp oil
1 medium-sized onion, finely chopped
1 × 400g can butter beans
1 large carrot, chopped or sliced into discs
2 medium-sized potatoes, peeled and diced
1 parsnip, peeled and diced
1 tsp mixed dried herbs
1.3 litres stock, heated until hot
Salt and pepper
2 tbsp chopped fresh parsley

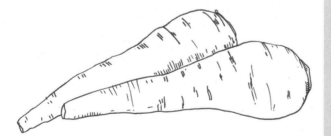

Sweet Potato

Ingredients:
15g butter or 2 tbsp oil
3 large sweet potatoes, diced
1 large potato, diced
1 onion, chopped finely
2 cloves garlic, chopped
1 × 400g can chickpeas
1 level tsp ground coriander
1 level tsp ground cumin
1.2 litres stock, heated unti hot
Salt and pepper to taste
1–2 tbsp coriander leaves, chopped

This lightly spiced soup is great for autumn evenings. I like to serve it with wholemeal toast.

1. Heat the cooker on high and add the butter or oil.

2. Add all the other ingredients except the stock, seasoning and coriander leaves. Stir well and cover. Cook for 30 minutes on high.

3. Stir in the stock and season to taste. Cover and cook for 5 hours on high or 7½ hours on low.

4. Stir in the coriander just before serving.

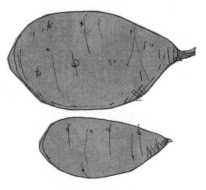

Vegetable Minestrone

Traditional minestrone is made with bacon stock and meat but this is an all-vegetable version. It is very good with lashings of Parmesan or Grana Padano cheese.

1. Heat the slow cooker on high and add the oil, onion, garlic, celery, carrot and tomatoes. Cover and leave to cook for 15 minutes.

2. Add the passata, cabbage, green beans, herbs and stock and season to taste.

3. Stir in the pasta, cover and cook on high for 4 ½ hours or on low for 7–7 ½ hours.

Ingredients:
2 tbsp olive oil
1 onion, chopped
1 clove garlic, chopped
1 stick celery, chopped
1 carrot, diced
6 ripe tomatoes, chopped
500ml passata
2 large green cabbage leaves, finely sliced
50g frozen, whole green beans, defrosted and cut into 2cm pieces
½ tsp dried thyme
½ tsp dried oregano
700ml stock, heated until hot
Salt and pepper to taste
100g pasta shapes

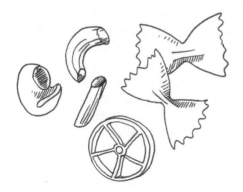

Onion

Ingredients:
7 medium-sized onions, white
Spanish onions give the best
flavour, red ones are much
sweeter. (Caramelise your onions
first if you wish – see
instructions.)
30g butter, melted prior to adding to
the cooker
Salt and black pepper
250ml dry, white wine
1.2 litres stock
2 tbsp freshly chopped parsley

This is the easiest of soups to prepare and makes a wonderful savoury treat. Serve with thick slices of French-style bread, covered with lashings of cheese and toasted under the grill.

1. Chop the onions finely. I tend to chop a couple by hand and pop the others in the food processor.

2. Heat the cooker on high and pour in the melted butter and onions. Season with salt and pepper to taste. Leave to cook for 20 minutes.

3. Heat the wine and the stock together and pour into the cooker over the onions. Stir and cover.

4. Leave to cook on high for 1 hour, then turn down to low and cook for 8 hours.

5. Stir in the parsley about 30 minutes before serving.

Caramelising onions
If you wish you can caramelise your onions in a frying pan before beginning to make the soup. Heat a little vegetable oil (approximately 1 tsp per onion) in a large frying pan, then add your onions. Turn the heat down to low and sprinkle a pinch of salt and ½ tsp sugar over the onions. Allow the onions to soften and release their sugars, turning them once or twice but no more. They will caramelise slowly over about 30 minutes. This process can be speeded up by cooking on a higher heat, but I find the flavour more bitter than sweet done this way. When they are the desired colour, add them to the slow cooker at the beginning of the recipe.

Carrot, Ginger and Coriander

I love carrot and coriander soup, but when the ginger is added it gets even better. Hot, buttered toast goes great with this soup.

Ingredients:
15g butter
1 onion
800g carrots, finely chopped or grated
1cm piece fresh ginger root, grated
1 tbsp coriander seeds, gently crushed
1.3 litres stock, heated until hot
Salt and pepper to taste
1-2 tbsp freshly chopped coriander leaves

1. Heat the cooker on high, adding the butter, whilst you finely chop the onion.

2. Stir the onion into the butter and add the carrots, ginger and coriander seeds. Stir well and cover. Leave to cook for 15 minutes.

3. Stir in the stock and season with salt and pepper.

4. Cover and cook on high for 4–4½ hours or on low for 7 hours.

5. Stir in the coriander leaves just before serving.

CHAPTER
3

Poultry and Game Soups

I make no excuses for the number of chicken recipes in this chapter. I love any chicken-based soup – it seems to be a cure all, but only if you use fresh chicken stock.

Whenever you eat chicken, always use the carcass and any leftover straggly bits to make stock. Nothing fancy, simply pour sufficient boiling water to cover the bones, season a little if you wish and simmer for 2 hours, checking the water level occasionally. Strain and use this stock to make soups. If you wish to store it, boil it down further to reduce. Keep your stock in a clean, lidded jar in the fridge for up to two weeks or freeze for four months.

If you do use a bought stock paste, cube or powder, make sure it is made from natural ingredients or your soup will taste very synthetic.

Economical Chicken Broth

This is one I cook regularly – it is tasty and very cheap to make.

1. Heat the slow cooker on high and add the butter, onion, garlic, carrots, celery and potato. Stir, then cover and leave to cook for 20 minutes.

2. Stir in the stock.

3. Add the rice and peas, stir in the herbs and season with salt and pepper to taste. Cover and cook for 3 hours on high or 5 hours on low.

4. Stir in the cooked chicken and parsley and cook for 1 more hour on high or 2 hours on low.

5. Serve with some warm soda bread and butter.

Ingredients:
15g butter
1 onion, finely chopped
1 clove garlic, chopped
2 large carrots, sliced into thin discs or diced
2 sticks celery, chopped
1 large potato, diced
1.2 litres chicken stock, heated until hot
3 tbsp long-grain rice
100g defrosted frozen or fresh peas
½ tsp dried sage or 2–3 fresh leaves, chopped
½ tsp dried tarragon
Salt and pepper to taste
200–250g cooked chicken, chopped
1–2 tbsp freshly chopped parsley

Creamy Chicken

Ingredients:
10g butter
3 shallots, finely chopped
2 cloves garlic, chopped
Juice of 1 lemon
800ml chicken stock. (For best results, use only homemade stock for this recipe.)
200ml whole milk
¼ tsp freshly grated nutmeg
½ tsp dried parsley
Salt and pepper to taste
200–250g cooked chicken, chopped
150ml single cream

Probably my favourite pick me up!

1. Heat the slow cooker on high and add the butter, shallots, garlic and lemon juice. Cover and cook for 20 minutes.

2. Heat the stock with the milk in a pan, bringing it to the boil. Then pour into the cooker.

3. Stir in the nutmeg and parsley and season to taste with salt and plenty of black pepper.

4. Cover and cook for 2 ½ hours on high or 4 hours on low.

5. Stir in the cooked chicken and cream and cook for 30 more minutes on high.

● **Poultry and Game Soups**

Chicken Noodle

I love the tasty runniness of this soup combined with the slippery noodles – have a napkin ready to wipe your chin!

1. Heat the cooker on high. Trim the chicken of any excess fat, but leave on the skin as it adds flavour to the soup.

2. Pour the two oils (or butter and sesame oil) into the cooker and add the onions. Cover and cook for 15 minutes.

3. Meanwhile, place the stock, wine or sherry, star anise, garlic, ginger and turmeric into a pan and bring to the boil. When it is boiling, pour over the onions in the cooker and place the chicken portions in the stock, making sure they are pressed well down.

4. Add the soy sauce. Cover and cook for 4 hours on high or 7½–8 hours on low, or until the chicken is tender.

5. Remove the chicken from the soup and cut the meat away from the bones and skin. Chop finely and put back into the soup.

6. Break up the noodles into the soup and stir. Cover and cook for 1 hour on high or 2 hours on low, or until the noodles are cooked to your liking.

7. Add a little more soy sauce to season if you wish. I like to serve this soup with thick slices of bread or hot, crispy spring rolls.

Ingredients:
4 chicken thighs, or 2 thighs and 2 drumsticks
1 tbsp vegetable oil or butter
1 tbsp sesame oil
5 spring onions, finely chopped. (Don't use too much of the green bit though – add this to another heartier soup.)
1.2 litres chicken stock, heated until hot
2 tbsp rice wine or dry sherry
1 star anise
1 clove garlic, chopped
2cm piece ginger root, grated
½ tsp turmeric
2 tbsp light soy sauce
350g fine egg noodles

Chicken with Spring Vegetables

Ingredients:
15g butter or 2 tbsp vegetable oil
1 leg and 1 breast of chicken, with bone left in
1 small onion, chopped
2 spring onions, chopped
4 spears asparagus, chopped into 2cm pieces
6 broccoli florets, quartered
6 small carrots, quartered or chopped
8 baby new potatoes, sliced or quartered
2 large spring cabbage leaves, finely sliced
1.3 litres chicken stock, heated until hot
1 garlic clove, chopped
½–1 tsp dried tarragon
Salt and pepper to taste
Small bunch watercress, coarsely chopped

A light, fresh tasting soup with the peppery addition of watercress.

1. Heat the slow cooker on high and add the butter or oil.

2. Trim any excess fat from the chicken portions.

3. Add the onion, spring onions, asparagus, broccoli, carrots, potatoes and cabbage to the cooker and stir well.

4. Pour in the stock and stir in the garlic and tarragon. Season to taste.

5. Place the chicken portions in the stock, making sure they are covered.

6. Cover and cook for 4 ½ hours on high or 8 hours on low.

7. Remove the chicken portions and strip the meat from the bones and skin, then add it back to the soup.

8. Stir in the watercress. Cover and cook for 30–40 minutes on high.

Lemony Chicken

A real treat for lemon chicken lovers.

1. Heat the cooker on high and add the butter or oil.

2. Trim any excess fat from the thighs. Loosen the flesh from the skin and place a slice of lemon under the skin, or for a lighter lemon flavour squeeze the juice directly onto the flesh under the skin. Leave to one side.

3. Put the onion and carrots in the cooker, cover and cook for 20 minutes.

4. Pour in the stock with the parsley and rice and stir well.

5. Add the chicken thighs, making sure they are well submerged in the stock. Season to taste.

6. Cover and cook on high for 4½–5 hours or 7½–8 hours on low.

7. Add the mushrooms after 3 hours on high or 5 hours on low. Continue cooking.

8. Remove the chicken from the soup and take the meat away from the bones, skin and lemon. Place back in the soup with the cream and stir.

9. Cook on high for 30–40 minutes.

10. Stir in the fresh parsley just before serving.

Ingredients:
15g butter or 2 tbsp vegetable oil
6 chicken thighs
2 lemons, each cut into 3 thick slices
1 onion, finely chopped
2 carrots, finely chopped
1 litre chicken stock, heated until hot
1 tsp dried parsley
2 tbsp long-grain rice
Salt and pepper to taste
50g button mushrooms, sliced
150ml single cream
1 tbsp freshly chopped parsley

Chicken and Sweetcorn

Ingredients:
15g butter or 2 tbsp vegetable oil
6 chicken thighs
1 onion, finely chopped
1 large potato, diced
1 red pepper, chopped
2 sticks celery, finely chopped
2 tbsp long-grain rice
1.2 litres chicken stock, heated until hot
250g fresh sweetcorn kernels cut away from the husk or defrosted frozen
Salt and pepper to taste
80ml double cream (optional)

These two ingredients go so well together. This soup is good and still filling without the cream, if you prefer a lighter version.

1. Heat the cooker on high and add the butter or oil. Cover.

2. Trim any excess fat from the chicken thighs.

3. Add the onion, potato, pepper, celery and rice to the cooker. Stir in the stock and sweetcorn. Season to taste.

4. Place the chicken portions in the stock making sure they are submerged.

5. Cover and cook on high for 4 ½ hours or on low for 7 hours.

6. Remove the meat from the bones and skin and chop well. Place back in the soup and stir in the cream. Cover and cook on high for 45 minutes.

Autumn Chicken

The apples and cider make a wonderful marriage with the chicken, giving a very autumnal flavour.

Ingredients:
15g butter or 2 tbsp vegetable oil
4 boneless chicken thighs, chopped
1 onion, finely chopped
1 litre chicken stock
200ml dry cider
Salt and pepper to taste
2 Bramley apples, peeled and diced
  (Place in cold water with a
  squeeze of lemon to stop them
  discolouring.)
¼–½ tsp ground cinnamon
½ tsp dried sage
2 bay leaves

1. Heat the slow cooker on high and add the butter or oil. Add the chicken, onion and a little of the stock. Cover and cook for 1 hour. Alternatively, place the butter or oil in a frying pan and fry the chicken and onion for 3–4 minutes before placing in the slow cooker.

2. Heat the stock and cider together until boiling then pour over the chicken and onion mixture. Season to taste.

3. Stir in the apples, cinnamon, sage and bay leaves. Cover and cook on high for 4 ½–5 hours or on low for 7 ½–8 hours.

Chicken and Mushroom

Ingredients:
15g butter or 2 tbsp oil
6 chicken thighs
1 onion, finely chopped
2 cloves garlic, chopped
Juice of 1 lemon
125ml dry white wine
1 tsp paprika
1 level tsp dried mixed herbs
750ml chicken stock, heated until hot
150g mushrooms, sliced or chopped
200ml single cream or full-fat natural
   yogurt for a tangier flavour

You could also use this recipe to fill a pie – simply use less stock and sprinkle 2 tsp plain flour to the mixture at stage 3.

1. Heat the slow cooker on high and add the butter or oil.

2. Trim any excess fat from the chicken and place in the cooker.

3. Add the onion, garlic, lemon juice, wine, paprika and herbs and pour over 500ml of the stock. Stir well, cover and cook for 3 hours on high.

4. Add the mushrooms and the rest of the stock. Cover and cook for 2 ½ hours on high or 5 hours on low.

5. Remove the chicken and cut the meat away from the bones and skin. Chop and place back in the cooker.

6. Stir in the cream or yogurt, cover and cook on high for 30–40 minutes.

7. Serve with some garlic croutons.

● **Poultry and Game Soups**

Italian Chicken

This is a recipe I have developed from a pasta sauce I make regularly. It isn't a true Italian recipe; that's just what my family like to call it.

1. Heat the slow cooker on high and add the oil.

2. Stir the onion, garlic, celery, carrot, chicken and tomato purée into the oil and pour over the tomatoes and wine. Stir well and cover and cook for 2 hours on high.

3. Stir in the stock, oregano and thyme and season to taste. Cook for 3 ½ hours on high or 5–6 hours on low.

4. Serve with some fresh basil leaves and toasted bruschetta slices brushed with olive oil.

Ingredients:
2 tbsp olive oil
1 small onion, finely chopped
2 cloves garlic
1 stick celery, finely chopped
1 carrot, finely chopped
2 boneless chicken breasts, chopped, or 350g minced chicken
2 tbsp tomato purée
1 × 400g can chopped tomatoes
100ml dry white wine
700ml chicken stock, heated until hot
½ tsp dried oregano
A few sprigs fresh thyme or ½ tsp dried
Salt and pepper to taste
Fresh basil to serve

Curried Chicken

Ingredients:
15g butter
4 chicken thighs
1 onion, finely chopped
1 red pepper, chopped
1 courgette, chopped
1 carrot, chopped
3 cloves garlic, chopped
2 tbsp curry powder, whichever
   strength you choose
1 litre chicken stock
250ml coconut milk
50g fresh or defrosted frozen peas
50g defrosted chopped green beans
2 tbsp freshly chopped coriander
   leaves

This can be as spicy as you wish – simply use either mild, medium or hot curry powder. It is a really easy, flavoursome soup.

1. Heat the slow cooker on high and add the butter.

2. Trim any excess fat off the chicken thighs.

3. Add all the vegetables, garlic and curry powder to the cooker.

4. Place the chicken thighs in the pot amongst the vegetables.

5. Combine the stock and coconut milk and heat to boiling, then pour over the chicken and vegetables. Cover and cook for 3 hours on high or 5 ½ hours on low.

6. Stir in the peas and beans and cover and cook for 2 ½ hours on high or 4 hours on low.

7. Just before serving, stir in the fresh coriander. Serve with strips of hot naan bread.

● **Poultry and Game Soups**

Creamy Chicken and Leek

A rich soup that is an ideal cold weather warmer.

1. Heat the slow cooker on high, adding the butter.

2. Add the leeks and potato and season with a little salt. Cover and cook for 15 minutes.

3. Add the chicken meat and the rest of the ingredients, except for the cream or milk. Stir well.

4. Cover and cook for 4 ½ hours on high or 7 hours on low.

5. Heat the cream or milk in a pan until almost boiling and stir into the soup. Cover and cook on high for 30 minutes.

6. Serve with some soda bread.

Ingredients:
20g butter
2 large leeks, chopped
1 large potato, diced
Salt to season
400g minced chicken or chopped thigh meat
1 litre chicken stock, heated until hot
½ tsp dried thyme
1 tsp black peppercorns, cracked in a pestle and mortar
200ml single cream or whole milk

Turkey with Winter Vegetables

Ingredients:
15g butter or 2 tbsp vegetable oil
1 large onion, finely chopped
1 small leek, finely chopped
2 large carrots, finely diced
200g swede, finely diced
1 large parsnip, finely chopped
2 medium-sized potatoes, diced
½ tsp dried thyme
½ tsp dried sage
Salt and pepper (White pepper is
    particularly good in this recipe.)
1.3 litres turkey stock, heated until
    hot
500g cooked turkey meat

I always have gallons of wonderful turkey stock left over from Christmas – I tend to freeze it in batches so I can use it through the following month. It never lasts long. The secret to this soup's flavour, apart from the stock, is the hour cooking the vegetables before adding the stock.

1. Heat the slow cooker on high and add the butter or oil.

2. Add the all the prepared vegetables and herbs and season with salt and pepper. Stir everything well and cover. Cook for 1 hour on high.

3. Add the stock and cook for 3 hours on high or 6 hours on low.

4. Stir in the cooked turkey and cook on high for 30 more minutes.

5. I like to serve this with some spicy potato wedges or crusty bread.

● **Poultry and Game Soups**

Thai-style Turkey

I had some delicious chicken soup in a Thai restaurant a while back and decided to try it with turkey.

Ingredients:
15g butter or vegetable oil
1 small onion or 4 spring onions, finely chopped
100g bok choy, finely shredded
1 small red pepper, finely sliced
1 lemongrass stalk, mince the lower portion or chop finely, and reserve the rest
2 tbsp green curry paste
1 tbsp fish sauce
1 dessertspoon brown sugar
800ml turkey stock
400ml coconut milk
2 kaffir lime leaves
300–350g cooked turkey, chopped
1 tbsp fresh coriander leaves
200g egg or rice noodles (optional)

1. Heat the slow cooker on high and add the butter or oil.

2. Place the vegetables, minced or chopped lemongrass, curry paste, fish sauce and brown sugar in the cooker and stir well. Cover and cook for 25 minutes.

3. Heat the stock and coconut milk together and stir into the other ingredients.

4. Add the lime leaves and the rest of the lemongrass stalk. Cover and cook for 3 ½ hours on high or 6 hours on low.

5. Stir in the cooked turkey and coriander leaves and cook on high for 30 minutes.

6. If you wish, you can add 200g egg or rice noodles to the cooker about 40 minutes before the cooking is finished on high or 1 hour before cooking is finished on low.

Turkey Chowder

Ingredients:
20g butter
1 small onion, finely chopped
2 carrots, sliced into thin discs
2 sticks celery, chopped
2 large potatoes, diced
1 red pepper, chopped
250g sweetcorn, fresh from the husk
   or defrosted frozen
Salt and pepper
1.2 litres turkey stock, heated until
   hot
½–1 tsp cayenne pepper, depending
   on how big a kick you want your
   soup to have
400–450g cooked turkey, chopped
50ml single cream

This is a real treat especially if, like me, you adore sweetcorn. It is a rich soup that warms and satisfies when you are hungry.

1. Heat the slow cooker on high and add the butter.

2. Add all the prepared vegetables and season with salt and pepper. Cover and cook on high for 20 minutes.

3. Pour in the stock and stir in the cayenne pepper.

4. Cover and cook for 3 ½ hours on high or 6 ½ hours on low.

5. Stir in the turkey and cream. Cover and cook on high for 30 more minutes.

● **Poultry and Game Soups**

Duck with Oyster Sauce

I love Chinese food and have adapted this recipe based on one of my local takeaway dishes. Take care with any extra seasoning as the oyster and soy sauces are very salty.

1. Heat the slow cooker on high and add 1 tbsp of the sunflower oil and the sesame oil.

2. Stir the onions and garlic into the oils and cover and cook for 20 minutes on high.

3. Add the other tablespoon of sunflower oil to a frying pan on your hob. Fry the duck breast skin-side down for 3–4 minutes until browned and then fry the underside very quickly. Leave to rest for a few minutes, then slice into thin strips.

4. Add a little stock to the frying pan and pour into the cooker. Place the meat in the cooker with the onions.

5. Stir the oyster and soy sauces and the wine into the rest of the hot stock and pour into the cooker.

6. Add the mushrooms and cover and cook for 3½ hours on high or 6½–7 hours on low.

Ingredients:
2 tbsp sunflower oil
½ tbsp sesame oil
5 spring onions, sliced into little strips
1 small onion, finely chopped
2 cloves garlic, finely chopped
1 large duck breast
1 litre poultry stock, heated until hot
4 tbsp oyster sauce
1 tbsp soy sauce
125ml dry white wine
80g mushrooms, any type will do so long as they are not too big

Duck

Not the title of the Marx Brothers' film, but a very tasty way to make duck go further. Duck and peas are a traditional duo.

Ingredients:
1 tbsp sunflower oil
2 large duck legs
1 onion, finely sliced
4 rashers lean bacon, chopped
1 litre poultry stock
150ml red wine
100g defrosted frozen peas

1. Heat the conventional oven to 200°C/Gas Mark 6. Place the oil and the duck legs in a roasting pan and roast for 20–25 minutes or until they turn golden brown. Leave to cool slightly.

2. Heat the cooker on high and add the onion, bacon and any fat or juices from roasting the duck legs. Add a little stock to loosen any debris in the roasting pan.

3. Heat the stock and wine together until boiling and pour into the cooker.

4. Add the duck legs and peas and cover and cook for 4 hours on high or 7 ½ hours on low.

Rabbit with Herb Dumplings

A family recipe from my relatives in Southport, though it was cooked on the hob. They were plagued by rabbits on their land . . . well they grew cabbages and sprouts, a bunny feast.

1. Heat the slow cooker on high and add the oil, the vegetables and the rabbit meat. Stir well and cover and cook for 45 minutes.

2. Heat the stock, stir in the redcurrant jelly and add the wine. Pour over the meat and vegetables. Add the tarragon and season to taste.

3. Stir in the rice and cover. Cook for 4 hours on high or 7½ hours on low.

4. Make the dumplings an hour before the cooking time is finished. If cooking on low, turn your slow cooker up to high when you begin to prepare the dumplings. Sieve the flour, salt and mustard into a bowl and stir in the herbs and suet. Mix in 5 tsp water and use a knife to bring the dough together. Keep adding 1 tsp water at a time until the dough is soft and slightly sticky. Flour your hands and roll the dough into balls about the size of a walnut.

5. Quickly drop the dumplings into the soup and replace the cover. Leave to cook for about 45–50 minutes on high or until the dumplings are light and fluffy. Don't remove the lid for at least 45 minutes.

Ingredients:
2 tbsp vegetable oil
2 large carrots, diced or thinly sliced
1 onion, chopped
2 sticks celery, chopped
1 leek, chopped
350–400g rabbit meat, chopped
1.2 litres poultry or rabbit stock, heated until hot
1 tablespoon redcurrant jelly
100ml white wine
1 tsp dried tarragon
Salt and pepper to taste
100g long-grain rice

For the dumplings:
100g self-raising flour
Pinch salt
½ tsp mustard powder
½ tsp dried parsley
½ tsp dried tarragon
50g suet, beef or vegetarian
Water to mix

Game

Ingredients:
15g butter
1 large onion, chopped
1 leek, chopped
2 carrots, chopped
100g swede, chopped
1 stick celery, chopped and save the leaves
4 rashers lean bacon, chopped
50g chicken livers, chopped (optional)
1 litre game stock, heated until hot
200ml red wine
2 tbsp port
1 tbsp fresh parsley
½ tsp dried mixed herbs
8-10 black peppercorns, crushed or roughly ground
Salt to taste
200-250g cooked game meat, chopped

This is not one I make very often, but it uses up all the last bits of game that would otherwise be thrown away. Make a stock from the carcasses or bones of rabbit, hare, pheasant, pigeon, partridge or venison. Pour boiling water over the bones and simmer for 3–4 hours, keeping an eye on the water levels. Drain the stock into a clean pan and boil for about 12–15 minutes to reduce slightly.

1. Heat the slow cooker on high and add the butter.

2. Add all the vegetables and bacon. Add the chicken livers if you want to bring a really rich flavour to the soup. Cover and cook for 30 minutes.

3. Combine the stock, wine and port. Stir into the cooker.

4. Add the herbs, celery leaves, peppercorns and salt to taste.

5. Cover and cook for 3 hours on high or 6 hours on low.

6. Stir in the cooked meat and cook for 30 more minutes on high.

Pheasant

When we were given a bird by some friends, I pondered over the size of it in terms of feeding five people. This is what I made – it is very special.

Ingredients:
2 tbsp vegetable oil and a knob of
  butter
1 pheasant
1 large onion, roughly chopped
1 large carrot, sliced into thin discs
2 large, dark green cabbage leaves,
  thinly shredded
3 sprigs fresh thyme or 1 tsp dried
2 bay leaves
2 good heads of parsley, chopped
1 litre poultry stock
200ml red wine
1 tbsp brandy
5 juniper berries (optional)
White pepper and salt to taste

1. Heat the slow cooker on high and add the oil and butter.

2. Place the pheasant in the cooker and surround it with the vegetables and herbs.

3. Put the stock in a pan with the wine and brandy and bring to the boil.

4. Pour the stock over the ingredients in the cooker, add the juniper berries if using, and season to taste. Cover and cook for 5 ½ hours on high or 8 hours on low.

5. Remove the pheasant and place in a dish so as to retain any juices and carefully remove all the meat. Return it back to the cooker. Cover and cook for 30 more minutes.

Scottish-style Venison

Ingredients:
2 tbsp vegetable oil or 15g butter
1 onion, chopped
3 carrots, chopped
2 small turnips, chopped
350g venison meat, chopped into
    small pieces
1.3 litres stock, poultry or venison,
    heated until hot
80g pearl barley
50g fresh nettle tops or spinach
    leaves
Salt and black pepper

We had a soup similar to this one in Wales actually.
A Scottish couple who ran a B&B served us this incredibly
delicious soup for lunch.

1. Heat the cooker on high and add the oil or butter.

2. Add the vegetables, apart from the nettles or
   spinach, and meat and stir well. Cover and cook for
   30 minutes.

3. Add the stock and stir in the barley. Cover and
   cook for 4 hours on high or 7½ hours on low.

4. Chop the nettles or spinach and add to the cooker.
   Leave for 15 more minutes on high.

Beef and Lamb Soups

So long as you have good quality stock, you don't need much meat to make these soups really tasty.

Bones make excellent stock very cheaply and your butcher will probably give you some lamb or beef bones free of charge or for a nominal amount. Simply pour boiling water over them, season with a little salt and pepper and add a few herbs if you wish, though herbs will be added in each soup recipe. Simmer for at least 2½ hours, topping up the water as necessary.

Economical Beef and Vegetable

Ingredients:
2 tbsp vegetable oil or 15g butter
1 onion, finely chopped
2 carrots, diced
2 sticks celery, chopped
150g swede, diced
1 leek, chopped
1 medium potato, diced
250g shin beef
1.2 litres beef stock, heated until hot
1 level tsp dried thyme
1 level tsp dried parsley
100g defrosted frozen peas
Salt and pepper

You can use up any leftover gravy from a roast dinner in the stock to add flavour to this purse-loving recipe.

1. Heat the slow cooker on high and add the oil or butter.

2. Stir in all the vegetables, apart from the peas. Cover and cook for 25–30 minutes.

3. Trim any excess fat from the meat, but leave a little on for flavour. Chop into very small pieces and add to the cooker.

4. Stir in the stock and herbs. Cover and cook for 2 hours on high or 5 hours on low.

5. Add the peas, cover and cook for 2 ½ hours on high or 3 on low.

6. Serve with warm wholemeal soda bread and butter.

● **Beef and Lamb Soups**

Beef and Barley

A good thick soup that smells wonderful as it cooks.

1. Heat the slow cooker on high and add the oil.

2. Stir in the vegetables and garlic, cover and cook for 20 minutes.

3. Add the beef and hot stock.

4. Stir in the tomato purée, pepper, thyme, barley and lentils. Season with salt to taste.

5. Cover and cook for 5 hours on high or 8 ½ hours on low.

6. Stir in the fresh parsley just before serving. Cheese scones go so well with this and make it a very substantial meal.

Ingredients:
2 tbsp vegetable oil
1 onion, finely chopped
1 garlic clove, chopped
2 sticks celery, chopped
2 large carrots, chopped
350g shin beef
1.2 litres beef stock, heated until hot
1 tbsp tomato purée
¼–½ tsp white pepper
1 level tsp dried thyme
200g pearl barley
100g red lentils
Salt to taste
2 tbsp chopped fresh parsley

Chilli Beef

Ingredients:
1 tbsp vegetable oil
1 large onion, chopped
2–3 cloves garlic, chopped
1 red pepper, chopped
350g minced beef
½–1 tsp dried chilli flakes
2 tbsp sweet chilli sauce
1 level tsp ground cumin
1 × 400g can chopped tomatoes
800ml beef stock
1 × 400g can red kidney beans, drained
Salt to taste

I love chilli con carne and this is a recipe I adapted from that dish. It serves more people for less meat.

1. Heat the slow cooker on high and add the oil, onion, garlic and pepper.

2. Stir in the minced beef and chilli flakes, sweet chilli sauce and cumin. Cover and cook for 45 minutes.

3. Combine the tomatoes and stock and heat in a pan on your hob until almost boiling. Pour over the ingredients in the cooker. Stir in the kidney beans and add salt to taste. Cover and cook for 4½ hours on high or 7 hours on low.

4. Serve with slices of French bread or other crusty white bread and some grated cheddar cheese.

Caribbean Beef with Dumplings

A Manchester café serves this amazing soup. I have just about reproduced the flavour – boy, do they like to guard their recipes.

1. Heat the slow cooker on high and add the oil, onion, sweet potatoes, plantain and carrots. Cover and cook for 30 minutes.

2. Add the meat and stir in the hot stock.

3. Stir in the split peas, thyme and spring onions. Season to taste and cover and cook for 4 ½ hours on high or 7 hours on low.

4. Add the okra and continue to cook for 30 minutes on high whilst you make the dumplings.

5. Sieve the flour and salt together in a bowl and add the butter. Rub it lightly into the flour until it resembles breadcrumbs. Add the water 1 tbsp at a time and mix to a firm but pliable dough. Roll small pieces in your hands until they resemble small thin sausages. Drop into the cooker, evenly spacing them in the soup. Cook on high for 45 minutes.

Ingredients:
2 tbsp vegetable oil
1 large onion, finely chopped
2 large sweet potatoes, cut into small pieces
Approx. 300g ripe plantain flesh, chopped
2 large carrots, chopped
350g stewing beef, cut into small pieces
1.2 litres beef stock, heated until hot
150g split peas
3 sprigs fresh thyme
3 spring onions
Salt and pepper
5 okra, sliced into discs

For the dumplings:
100g self-raising flour
40g very cold butter, cut into small pieces
½ tsp salt
Water to mix

Beef and Tomato

Ingredients:
2 tbsp vegetable oil or 15g butter
1 onion, chopped
1 carrot, chopped
1 green pepper, chopped
1 large potato, diced
1 stick celery, chopped
400g braising steak, cut into small
    pieces
600ml beef stock
1 × 400g can chopped tomatoes
250ml passata
1 clove garlic, chopped
½ tsp salt
1 tsp brown sugar
1 level tsp paprika
½–1 tsp cayenne pepper
2 tbsp tomato purée
Black pepper to taste
2 bay leaves

This soup has a slight kick due to the cayenne pepper – the more you use the more it kicks.

1. Heat the slow cooker on high and add the oil or butter.

2. Add the onion, carrot, pepper, potato and celery and stir. Cover and cook for 20 minutes.

3. Add the meat.

4. Combine the stock, tomatoes and passata in a pan and heat to almost boiling, then pour into the cooker and stir well.

5. In a small dish, mix together the garlic, salt, brown sugar, paprika, cayenne, tomato purée and black pepper. Stir this into the soup.

6. Add the bay leaves, cover and cook for 5½ hours on high or 8½ hours on low.

7. Serve with some garlic and olive oil croutons.

Beef and Lamb Soups

Chinese-style Beef and Noodle

A real change from chicken noodle soup.

1. Heat the slow cooker on high and add the oil. Add all the ingredients listed from the spring onions to hoisin sauce and stir well.

2. Add the stock and stir.

3. Heat the vegetable and sesame oil mix in a frying pan and lightly fry the meat all over. Add to the cooker. Cover and cook for 5 hours on high or 7½ hours on low.

4. An hour before the end of the cooking time, break up the noodles and add to the cooker.

Ingredients:
1 tbsp vegetable oil
5 spring onions, chopped
3cm piece ginger, grated
4 cloves garlic, chopped
½ tsp five-spice powder
½ tsp chilli flakes
2 tbsp rice wine
2 tbsp dark soy sauce
1 tbsp hoisin sauce
1 litre beef stock, heated until hot
1 tbsp vegetable oil mixed with
    1 tbsp sesame oil
400g lean stewing beef (best
    braising steak is good for this),
    cut into thin strips
200g egg or rice noodles

Beef and Mushroom

Ingredients:
2 tbsp vegetable oil
3 rashers lean bacon, chopped
1 onion, chopped
1 clove garlic, chopped
400g lean braising steak, cut into strips
2 tbsp soy sauce
1 litre beef stock, heated until hot
1 tsp mixed herbs, either dried or as bouquet garni
1 bay leaf
100g long-grain rice
200g medium-sized mushrooms, sliced
4–5 tbsp sour cream, at room temperature

I love beef and mushrooms in anything and this soup is no exception.

1. Heat the slow cooker on high and add the oil, bacon, onion and garlic. Stir, cover and cook for 25 minutes.

2. Add the steak and soy sauce and stir in the stock.

3. Add the herbs and bay leaf and stir in the rice. Cover and cook for 5 hours on high or 8 hours on low.

4. Add the mushrooms half way through the cooking time.

5. Just before serving stir in the sour cream.

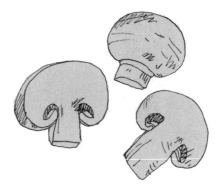

54

Curried Beef

Make this as spicy as you wish by using mild or spicier pastes.

1. Heat the slow cooker on high and add the oil and butter.

2. Combine the curry paste, tomato purée and boiling water together in a small jug.

3. Put the onion in the cooker and stir in the paste mixture.

4. Stir in the carrots, cauliflower and potato. Cover and cook for 30 minutes.

5. Add the meat and pour over the stock. Stir in the lentils and season to taste. Cover and cook for 5 hours on high or 8 hours on low.

6. Add the spinach and cook for 30 more minutes on high.

7. Serve with chapattis, naan or pitta bread.

Ingredients:
2 tbsp vegetable oil and a knob of butter
3 tbsp curry paste (rogan josh, balti, jalfrezi or Madras)
2 tbsp tomato purée
100ml boiling water
1 onion, chopped
2 carrots, chopped
6 cauliflower florets, each cut into 4 pieces
1 large potato, chopped
350g stewing beef, cut into small chunks
1.1 litres beef stock, heated until hot
150g red lentils
Salt to taste
6 sections of frozen spinach or 2 big handfuls fresh leaves

Beef and Lamb Soups ●

Beef and Bean

Ingredients:
2 tbsp oil
1 onion, chopped
1 stick celery, chopped
1 carrot, chopped
½ medium-sized aubergine, diced
1 clove garlic, chopped
1 tsp dried mixed herbs
350g minced steak
1.2 litres beef stock, heated until hot
1 × 300g can borlotti beans
1 × 300g can cannellini beans
100g defrosted green beans, cut into
    2cm pieces
50g barley
Salt and pepper to taste

This is quite a quick-cooking soup, even in the slow cooker. It is a thick, filling, main meal-style soup.

1. Heat the slow cooker on high and add the oil, onion, celery, carrot and aubergine.

2. Add the garlic and herbs and stir in the meat. Cover and cook for 1 hour on high.

3. Stir in the stock.

4. Drain the beans and stir into the soup with the defrosted green beans.

5. Add the barley and season with salt and pepper to taste.

6. Cover and cook on high for 3 hours or 5 ½ hours on low.

Beef and Ale

I love beef and ale pie, and was sure it would transform into a wonderfully flavoured soup. The secret is long, slow cooking.

1. Heat the slow cooker on high and add all the ingredients except for the ale and stock. Cover and cook for 1 hour on high.

2. Heat the ale and stock until boiling, then pour over the other ingredients.

3. Cover and cook on low for 7½–8½ hours.

Ingredients:
2 tbsp oil or 15g butter
1 onion, finely chopped
1 carrot, diced
1 clove garlic, chopped
8 baby new potatoes, halved
450g stewing beef, trimmed of
    excess fat and cut into small
    cubes
1 tsp dried or 3 sprigs fresh thyme
Salt and lots of white pepper
500ml ale (any type, but not too
    bitter)
700ml beef stock

Scotch Broth

Ingredients:
100g dried peas, soaked overnight
1 tbsp vegetable oil
1 onion, chopped
1 leek, chopped
3 carrots, diced or sliced
50g turnips, diced
2 sticks celery
½ tsp dried thyme or sprig of fresh
1.2 litres lamb stock, heated until
  boiling
100g pearl barley
Salt and pepper to taste
2 large lamb shoulder chops

A traditional soup using a recipe I got from a wonderful chef in Scotland. Though he makes it on the hob, it transfers very well to the slow cooker.

1. Heat the slow cooker on high and add the vegetable oil.

2. Drain the peas and rinse under cold water.

3. Add the vegetables and thyme to the cooker. Stir the peas into the boiling stock. Pour into the cooker. Stir in the barley and season to taste.

4. Put the lamb into the soup making sure it is well submerged.

5. Cover and cook for 5 ½ hours on high or 8 ½ hours on low

6. Serve with soda bread or oat cakes.

Lamb with Herbs and Vegetables

For the best flavour, use a good, rich stock in this recipe.

Ingredients:
2 tbsp oil or 15g butter
1 onion, finely chopped
2 carrots, finely diced
200g swede, finely diced
350g lean lamb steak, cut into small
  pieces
1.2 litres lamb stock, heated until hot
1 sprig fresh rosemary
1 tbsp freshly chopped parsley
1 sprig thyme
8–10 mint leaves
Salt and pepper to taste
150g fresh or defrosted frozen peas
Extra tbsp freshly chopped parsley
  and a few more mint leaves to
  serve

1. Heat the slow cooker on high and add the oil or butter, onion, carrot and swede.

2. Stir in the lamb and add about 200ml of the hot stock. Cover and cook for 1 hour on high.

3. Add the rest of the stock and all the herbs. Season to taste and cover and cook for 3 ½ hours on high or 6 ½ hours on low.

4. Add the peas and cook on high for 1 ½ hours or 3 ½ hours on low.

5. Add the extra herbs just before serving. Serve with some crusty bread and butter.

Moroccan Lamb

Ingredients:
2 tbsp oil
1 onion, finely chopped
2 sticks celery, finely chopped
400g minced lamb
800ml lamb stock, heated until hot
½ tsp each ground ginger, cinnamon
    and cayenne pepper
1 tsp turmeric
1 tsp garlic purée
1 tbsp tomato purée
Juice of 1 lemon
1 × 400g can chopped tomatoes
100g fine spaghetti or similar pasta
1 × 400g can chickpeas
170g canned green lentils, drained

A gently spiced, flavour-rich soup.

1. Heat the slow cooker on high and add the oil, onion and celery.

2. Stir in the lamb and 200ml of the stock. Cover and cook for 30 minutes.

3. Mix all the spices, garlic purée, tomato purée and lemon juice together in a small dish and stir into the meat and vegetables.

4. Heat the remaining stock and tomatoes together and pour over the ingredients in the cooker. Cover and cook on high for 3 ½ hours or 5 ½ hours on low.

5. Break the spaghetti in half. Add the chickpeas, lentils and spaghetti to the cooker and stir well into the mixture.

6. Cover and cook for 2 hours on high or 4 hours on low.

7. Serve with fingers of wholemeal pitta bread.

Beef and Lamb Soups

Lamb Mulligatawny

This soup is normally made with beef, but I think it is even more delicious with lamb.

Ingredients:
20g butter
3 tbsp mild or medium curry powder
2 tsp turmeric
1 tsp paprika
1 onion, finely chopped
1 carrot, finely chopped
1 courgette, sliced into discs
400g minced lamb
1.2 litres lamb stock, heated until hot
Juice of 1 lemon
1 Bramley apple, diced
25g basmati rice
Salt to taste
1 tbsp freshly chopped coriander
   leaves
150ml full-fat yogurt, at room
   temperature

1. Heat the slow cooker on high and add the butter, curry powder, turmeric and paprika. Cover and cook for 15–20 minutes or until the butter just starts to melt.

2. Stir in the vegetables and the meat.

3. Add the stock, lemon juice, apple and rice and stir well. Season with salt to taste.

4. Cover and cook for 5 hours on high or 7 ½ hours on low.

5. Stir in the fresh coriander and yogurt just before serving. Serve with fresh, warm naan bread.

Turkish Lamb

Ingredients:
1 lamb shank
1 onion, finely chopped
2 carrots, finely diced
3 cloves garlic, chopped
2 tsp ground cumin
1 tsp ground coriander
½ tsp cayenne pepper
½ tsp chilli flakes
1 tsp dried mint
1 litre lamb stock
300ml passata
50g dried apricots, chopped
30g sultanas
Salt to taste
1 tbsp freshly chopped mint leaves

A slightly spicier soup than the Moroccan one, laced with mint. This recipe uses a lamb shank, but you can use 2 shoulder chops if you find it difficult to find the lamb shank.

1. Heat the slow cooker on high. Place the lamb shank and vegetables in the cooker.

2. Combine the spices and herbs and sprinkle over the meat.

3. Heat the stock and passata together until very hot and pour over the ingredients in the cooker.

4. Stir in the dried fruit and season to taste. Cover and cook on high for 6 ½ hours. This can be cooked on low but it takes around 9–10 hours to get the best flavour from the shank.

5. Remove the meat from the shank bone and place back in the soup. Stir in the mint. Cover and cook for 30 more minutes on high.

Variation
If you like a heartier soup, a 400g can of chickpeas may be added 2 hours before the end of the cooking time.

Lancashire Hot Pot

Cooking some crispy potato slices to go with this really makes it a treat.

1. Heat the slow cooker on high and add the butter.

2. Add all the ingredients, apart from the potatoes and oil, to the cooker, mixing well.

3. Cover and cook on high for 6 hours or on low for 8 hours.

4. About 40 minutes before the end of the cooking time, remove any meat from the cutlets and place back in the cooker.

5. Preheat the oven to 200°C/Gas Mark 6. Drizzle a little oil on a baking sheet and spread the potatoes evenly over the sheet. Drizzle some more oil over them and season with a pinch of salt. Cook for about 30 minutes or until golden and crispy.

6. To serve, top each bowlful of soup with some of the crispy potato slices.

Ingredients:
15g butter
1 large onion, chopped
3 carrots, sliced into discs
2 large potatoes, cubed
300g lamb shoulder meat, cubed
2 lamb cutlets
1 lamb's kidney, chopped
2 tsp Worcestershire sauce
1 litre stock, heated until hot
2 bay leaves
½ tsp dried thyme
Salt and white pepper to taste
2 large potatoes, thickly sliced
Oil to crisp the potatoes

Lamb with Spring Cabbage

Ingredients:
2 tbsp vegetable oil
1 onion, finely chopped
1 clove garlic, chopped
350g lamb steak, cut into small cubes
1.2 litres lamb stock, heated until hot
1 sprig rosemary or 1 tsp dried
80g pearl barley
8 small new potatoes, cut into slices
Salt and pepper to taste
3-4 spring cabbage leaves, shredded
   finely
50g defrosted frozen peas
Mint leaves to serve (optional)

This is one of my favourite meals in a soup bowl.

1. Heat the slow cooker on high and add the oil, onion and garlic.

2. Add the lamb and the hot stock.

3. Add the rosemary, barley and potatoes. Season with salt and pepper. Cover and cook on high for 4½ hours or 6½ hours on low.

4. Add the cabbage and peas. Cover and cook for 1½ hours on high or 3 hours on low.

5. Just before serving, add a few mint leaves if you wish.

Lamb with Lentils and Peas

The touch of cumin really adds something to the flavour of this soup.

1. Heat the slow cooker on high and add the butter or oil, onion, garlic, carrots and lamb. Stir well.

2. Mix the tomato purée, cumin, stock and red wine together and pour over the meat and vegetables.

3. Stir in the peas and lentils and season to taste. Cover and cook on high for 4½–5 hours or 7½–8 hours on low.

4. Serve with some crusty bread and butter.

Ingredients:
15g butter or 2 tbsp vegetable oil
1 onion, finely chopped
2 cloves garlic
2 carrots, chopped
400g lamb shoulder steak, cut into small pieces
3 tbsp tomato purée
2 tsp ground cumin
1 litre lamb stock, heated until hot
150ml red wine
100g split peas
120g red lentils
Salt and pepper to taste

Basque Lamb

A deliciously garlic-laden soup from the Basque region of France. It is traditionally made with just lamb bones and cooked for hours on an open fire. Here, it is still cooked for hours but in a slow cooker!

Ingredients:
15g butter
1 onion, finely sliced
1 large red pepper, sliced
3 large beef tomatoes, chopped
7 cloves garlic, chopped
400g lamb shoulder steak, chopped
2 tbsp freshly chopped parsley
200ml red wine
900ml lamb stock, heated until hot
2 tsp paprika
1 bay leaf
Salt and pepper to taste

1. Heat the slow cooker on high and add all the ingredients together.

2. Cover and cook on high for 1 hour or on low for 7½–8 hours.

3. Serve with French bread torn into small pieces and added to the soup.

Beef and Lamb with Butterbeans

I like the mixture of beef and lamb together and often mix them in a hot pot.

1. Heat the slow cooker on high and add the butter or oil.

2. Add the onion, celery and garlic. Then add the minced beef and lamb cutlets.

3. Combine the passata and stock and heat together to almost boiling. Pour over the ingredients in the cooker.

4. Drain the beans, rinse in cold water and add them to the cooker.

5. Stir in the herbs and black pepper and season with salt. Cover and cook on high for 5 ½ hours or 7 ½ hours on low.

6. Remove the meat from the cutlets and place back in the cooker. Cook for 1 hour on high.

Ingredients:
100g dried butterbeans, soaked in cold water overnight
15g butter or 2 tbsp vegetable oil
1 onion, finely chopped
2 sticks celery, chopped
2 cloves garlic, chopped
300g minced beef
2 lamb cutlets
500ml passata
700ml beef or lamb stock
½ tsp each oregano, thyme and black pepper
Salt to taste

CHAPTER
5

Ham and Pork Soups

Ham hocks and pig's trotters make wonderful bases for soups and stews. They cost very little – we get ours from our local market. They can be frozen so buy a few, then you always have available the base for a good, hearty meal when pennies are few.

Two pig's trotters simmered for 2½ hours makes an excellent stock for soup and pork pies. They make about four portions of well-flavoured stock, which can be frozen separated into batches.

If you don't have any hock or trotter stock, use chicken stock or a good quality chicken or vegetable stock cube or paste.

I know there seems to be a lot of pea-based recipes in this chapter, but each soup uses a different type of pea and they are quite delicious!

Ham Hock and Pea

This is a family favourite. Great for cold, winter evenings.

1. Heat the slow cooker on high and put the ham hock in the base.

2. Add the onion, carrots and herbs. Pour over the stock.

3. Drain the peas and add to the pot. Season to taste and stir well.

4. Cover and cook on high for 6 ½ hours or until the hock is tender and the peas are cooked.

5. Remove all the meat from the hock, chop into small pieces and place back in the cooker. Cover and cook on high for 30 more minutes.

6. Serve with potato wedges or homemade chips, or simply some bread.

Ingredients:
1 ham hock. (Ask the butcher if it is necessary to soak it in cold water to remove some of the salt.)
1 large onion, finely chopped
3 large carrots, diced
1 tsp dried mixed herbs
1.3 litres pork stock or water, heated until hot
200g dried marrowfat peas, soaked in cold water overnight
Salt and pepper to taste

Bacon and Cauliflower

Ingredients:
20g butter
1 small onion, finely chopped
1 leek, finely chopped
4 large rashers back bacon, chopped
500g cauliflower florets, cut into
   bite-sized pieces
150ml single cream
1 tbsp freshly chopped parsley
2–3 rashers streaky bacon, fried or
   grilled until crisp, and then
   chopped

These two ingredients make a tasty combination.

1. Heat the slow cooker on high and add the butter, onion, leek and bacon. Add the stock and season to taste. Stir well and cover and cook on high for 30 minutes.

2. Stir in the cauliflower and hot stock and season to taste. Cover and cook on high for 4 ½ hours or 7 hours on low.

3. Stir in the cream and parsley. Cover and cook on high for 20 more minutes.

4. Serve topped with the crispy bacon.

Lentil and Bacon

I like this with lots of black pepper.

1. Heat the slow cooker on high and add the butter or oil.

2. Add the onion, bacon and garlic. Cover and cook on high for 30 minutes.

3. Stir in the carrots and lentils.

4. Stir the tomato purée into the hot stock and pour over the cooker ingredients. Stir in the passata or can of tomatoes and season with salt and plenty of black pepper.

5. Cover and cook for 5 hours on high or 7 ½ hours on low.

6. Serve with crusty bread or warm soda bread.

Ingredients:
15g butter or 2 tbsp vegetable oil
1 onion, finely chopped
6 rashers smoked, streaky bacon, chopped
1 clove garlic, chopped
2 large carrots, grated
200g red lentils
2 tbsp tomato purée
1.2 litres stock, heated until hot
300ml passata or 1 × 200g can chopped tomatoes
Salt and black pepper to taste

Pork with Mixed Vegetables

Ingredients:
15g butter, melted
1 onion, chopped
1 leek, chopped
2 carrots, chopped
100g swede, diced
1 medium-sized potato, diced
1 sweet potato, diced
400g pork shoulder steak, chopped
 into small pieces
1.3 litres stock, heated until hot
1 tsp mixed dried herbs
80g long-grain rice
Salt and pepper

A complete meal in one go.

1. Heat the slow cooker on high and add the butter, vegetables and meat. Stir well.

2. Add the stock, herbs and rice and season to taste.

3. Cover and cook for 4 ½ hours on high or 7 hours on low.

4. Serve with some crusty bread.

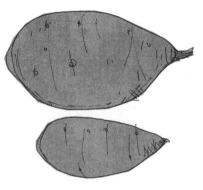

Leek and Bacon

Leeks are fantastic for soup making – I always have a couple waiting to be made into soup.

1. Heat the slow cooker on high and add the butter.

2. Add the onion, leeks and bacon and stir into the butter. Cover and cook for 30 minutes on high.

3. Stir in the potatoes and stock and add the rosemary. Season to taste. Cover and cook for 4 ½ hours on high or 7 ½ hours on low.

4. 40 minutes before the end of cooking, stir in the cream.

5. This is a very filling soup but it goes well with some wholemeal toast.

Ingredients:
15g butter
1 small onion, finely chopped
2 leeks, chopped
6 rashers streaky bacon, unsmoked or smoked, chopped
2 medium-sized potatoes, diced
1.2 litres stock, heated until hot
1 sprig rosemary
Salt and pepper to taste
150ml single cream

Split Pea and Ham

Ingredients:
15g butter
1 onion, finely chopped
2 sticks celery, chopped
2 carrots, chopped
120g split peas
1.2 litres stock, heated until hot
Salt and pepper to taste
250-300g cooked ham, cubed
2 tbsp fresh parsley or 2 tsp dried
1 tbsp chopped fresh chives

I often make this when I have boiled a ham. I use the cooking water for the stock, if it isn't too salty, and add cubes of the leftover meat.

1. Heat the slow cooker on high and add the butter and all the vegetables. Add the stock and seasoning. Stir well.

2. Cover and cook for 4½–5 hours on high or 7–7½ hours on low.

3. 30 minutes before the end of the cooking time, stir in the ham, parsley and chives.

Fresh (or Frozen) Pea and Ham

This is a summer soup, when fresh peas may be had, but it can be made any year round with the wonderful frozen pea.

1. Heat the slow cooker on high and add the butter and oil.

2. Add the shallots and peas and season with salt and pepper. Cover and cook for 20 minutes.

3. Add the stock and stir in the chives. Cover and cook on high for 3 hours.

4. Add the cooked ham and cover and cook for 45 minutes on high.

5. Add some fresh mint leaves to serve.

Ingredients:
25g butter and 1 tbsp sunflower oil. (This gives the best flavour.)
5 shallots, finely chopped
600g freshly podded peas or defrosted frozen peas
Salt and pepper to taste
1.2 litres stock, heated until hot
2 tbsp freshly chopped chives
300g cooked ham, chopped
Some fresh mint leaves to serve

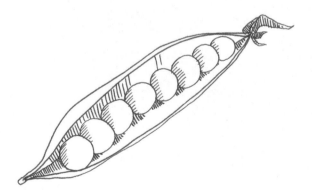

Ham and Bean

Ingredients:

200g dried butterbeans, soaked overnight in cold water
1 ham hock
1 onion, finely chopped
2 sticks celery, chopped
2 carrots, chopped
1 clove garlic, chopped
1.3 litres stock or water, heated until hot
1 tsp mustard powder
½ tsp white pepper
2 bay leaves

I tend to make this with butterbeans, but any dried white bean will do, cannellini or borlotti for example.

1. Heat the slow cooker on high and add the ham hock.

2. Add all the vegetables, including the drained beans and garlic. Stir in the stock.

3. Combine the mustard and pepper and sprinkle over the soup ingredients. Stir well.

4. Add the bay leaves and cover and cook for 5 ½ hours.

5. Cut the meat from the bone and place back in the soup. Stir well and cook for 30 more minutes.

6. Serve with wholemeal bread and butter.

● **Ham and Pork Soups**

Chinese Pork and Noodle

This is a quick-cooking soup even in the slow cooker.

1. Heat the slow cooker on high.

2. Heat the two oils together in a frying pan and add the five-spice powder and black bean sauce. Fry the pork for 3–4 minutes, then add to the slow cooker.

3. Add the spring onions, pak choy, ginger, garlic and chilli. Stir in the stock and soy sauce.

4. Cover and cook for 3 hours on high.

5. Add the noodles and cover and cook for 40 minutes on high.

6. I like to eat this soup with prawn toast.

Ingredients:
2 tbsp vegetable oil
1 tbsp sesame oil
1 tsp five-spice powder
1 tbsp black bean sauce
400g pork tenderloin, cut into little strips
5 spring onions, chopped
200g pak choy, sliced or shredded
3cm piece root ginger, grated
3 cloves garlic, chopped
1 green chilli, sliced
1.2 litres stock, heated until hot
2 tbsp soy sauce
150g egg noodles

Pork and Courgette

Ingredients:
2 tbsp vegetable oil
1 onion, finely chopped
1 clove garlic, chopped
2 pork chops, trim off excess fat
1 green pepper, sliced and chopped
3 medium-sized courgettes, chopped
5 sundried tomatoes in oil from a jar, chopped
1 × 400g can chopped tomatoes
800ml stock, heated until hot
1 tsp dried oregano
½ tsp dried sage
Salt and pepper to taste
1 tbsp freshly chopped parsley

I like to use pork chops in this recipe as the bones give an extra meaty flavour, but you can use pork shoulder if you wish.

1. Heat the slow cooker on high. Add 1 tbsp of the oil and add the onion and garlic.

2. Add the rest of the oil to a frying pan and cook the chops on both sides very lightly. Then sit the pork chops on top of the onions in the cooker.

3. Add all the other ingredients, apart from the parsley, and stir well. Season to taste.

4. Cover and cook on high for 5 hours or on low for 8 hours.

5. Remove the meat from the bones and place back in the soup. Stir in the fresh parsley and cook on high for 30 more minutes.

6. Serve with some garlic bread.

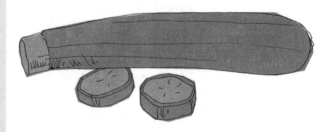

Pork with Mushrooms

Another quick-cooking soup.

Ingredients:
2 tbsp oil and a knob of butter
2 cloves garlic, chopped
1 onion, very finely chopped
450g lean minced pork
150g large mushrooms, chopped
150g button mushrooms, halved
1 litre stock, heated until hot
2 tbsp oyster sauce
Salt and pepper to taste
150ml single cream (optional)

1. Heat the slow cooker on high and add the oil, butter, garlic and onion. Cover and cook for 30 minutes.

2. Add the minced pork and both types of the mushrooms. Pour in the stock and oyster sauce and season to taste.

3. Cover and cook for 3 ½ hours on high or 5 ½ hours on low.

4. For an extra rich flavour, stir in the single cream 30 minutes before the end of the cooking time.

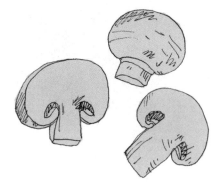

Ham and Pork Soups •

Mexican Pork

Ingredients:
2 tbsp vegetable oil
1 onion, finely chopped
1 clove garlic, chopped
3 green chillies, chopped
1 tsp dried oregano
450g minced pork
800ml stock
1 × 400g can chopped tomatoes
Salt to taste

This soup is based on a delicious stew we had at some friends' house last year. Neither of them are Mexican, however.

1. Heat the slow cooker on high and add the oil, onion and garlic. Cover and cook for 30 minutes.

2. Stir in the chillies, oregano and minced pork.

3. Heat the stock and tomatoes to boiling and then pour over the meat and onions. Season with salt to taste. Be careful with pepper – I find it affects the flavour of the chillies, so I don't add any to this dish.

4. Cover and cook on high for 4 hours or on low for 7½ hours.

Toulouse Sausage

Use the authentic Toulouse sausages for the best flavour.

1. Heat the slow cooker on high and add the oil, leek, garlic and bacon. Stir and cover and cook for 40 minutes.

2. Fry the sausages until lightly browned and then cut them into chunks. Add to the soup.

3. Put the stock, wine, chilli flakes and seasoning in a pan and bring to the boil. Pour into the cooker.

4. Cover and cook on high for 3 ½ hours.

5. Stir in the butterbeans and cook for 2 more hours on high or 5 hours on low.

6. Stir in the parsley just before serving.

Ingredients:
1 tbsp vegetable oil
1 large leek, chopped
1 clove garlic, chopped
4 rashers streaky bacon, chopped
6 Toulouse sausages
1 litre stock
200ml dry white wine
½ tsp chilli flakes
Salt and pepper to taste
1 × 400g can butterbeans, drained
2 tbsp freshly chopped parsley

Leek, Potato and Chorizo

Ingredients:
1 tbsp vegetable oil
1 onion, finely chopped
2 large leeks, chopped
2–3 cloves garlic, chopped
4 medium-sized potatoes, diced
200g chorizo, chopped
1.2 litres stock, heated until hot
½ tsp cayenne pepper, optional but
   gives an extra kick to the soup
Salt and pepper to taste

The flavour of the chorizo blends so well with the vegetables.

1. Heat the slow cooker on high and add the oil, onion, leeks, garlic and potatoes. Cover and cook for 1 hour on high.

2. Add the chorizo, stock, cayenne if using, and season with salt and pepper. Stir well.

3. Cover and cook on high for 3 ½ hours or on low for 6 ½ hours.

4. I like to serve this with cheese scones.

Polish Sausage

Use kabanos for this recipe – they can be bought quite easily in delicatessens or supermarkets.

Ingredients:
1 tbsp oil
1 onion, finely chopped
2 cloves garlic, chopped
3 carrots, chopped
200g Polish kabanos
1.2 litres stock, heated until hot
1 tsp paprika
1 sprig thyme or ½ tsp dried
100g brown long-grain rice
Salt and pepper to taste
3 large, dark green cabbage leaves or kale, shredded

1. Heat the slow cooker on high and add the oil, onion, garlic and carrots. Cover and cook for 20 minutes.

2. Chop the kabanos into small cubes or slice into quite thin discs. Add to the cooker.

3. Pour in the stock and stir in the paprika, thyme, rice and seasoning. Cover and cook for 3 hours on high or 5 ½ hours on low.

4. Stir in the cabbage or kale and cover and cook for 40 more minutes on high.

Pork Sausage and Lentil

Ingredients:
1 tbsp oil
1 onion, chopped
1 leek, chopped
1 stick celery, chopped
2 carrots, chopped
1 red pepper, chopped
1 clove garlic, chopped
2 tbsp tomato purée
1 tsp ground cumin
1 tsp dried thyme
1.2 litres stock, heated until hot
200g Puy lentils
6 pork sausages
Salt and pepper to taste

If you prefer to use low-fat sausages in this recipe, it is very successful.

1. Heat the slow cooker on high and add the oil, onion, leek, celery, carrots, pepper and garlic. Stir and cover and cook for 30 minutes.

2. Combine the tomato purée, cumin and thyme with the stock and pour over the vegetables. Stir in the lentils.

3. Cover and cook on high whilst you fry the sausages gently until brown all over. Cut the sausages into bite-sized pieces and add to the cooker.

4. Season with salt and pepper and cover and cook for 4 ½ hours on high or 7 hours on low.

● **Ham and Pork Soups**

Gammon and Chestnut

An interesting combination, ideal for a winter warming dish.

1. Heat the slow cooker on high and add the oil and vegetables. Cover and cook for 30 minutes.

2. Gently fry the gammon in a little oil if necessary and add to the cooker.

3. Add the chestnuts and hot stock. Stir in the thyme and salt and pepper to taste.

4. Cover and cook on high for 4 hours or low for 7½ hours.

5. Grill or fry the bacon until crispy and chop and sprinkle on the soup to serve.

Ingredients:
1 tbsp vegetable oil
1 onion, chopped
1 stick celery, chopped
2 carrots, chopped
1 gammon steak weighing about 200–250g, cubed
250g chestnuts, shells removed. (Score the chestnuts and place in a dish in the microwave for 2 minutes, remove the shells whilst still warm for ease. Halve them if you wish.)
1.2 litres stock, heated until hot
1 tsp dried thyme
Salt and pepper to taste
2 rashers streaky bacon

Satay Pork

Ingredients:
1 tbsp vegetable oil
1 tbsp sesame oil
3 spring onions, chopped
3 cloves garlic, chopped
1 red pepper, chopped
1 medium parsnip, grated
2cm piece ginger, grated
2 tbsp rice wine
2 tbsp honey
4 rounded tbsp crunchy peanut
  butter
400g minced pork
1.2 litres stock, heated until hot
1 tbsp soy sauce

I love satay sauce dishes and this is delicious.

1. Heat the slow cooker on high and add the two oils.

2. Stir in the onions, garlic, pepper, parsnip and ginger.

3. Put the rice wine, honey and peanut butter in a separate dish and stir in the pork. Mix well so the meat is coated in the flavours. Stir this into the cooker.

4. Pour over the stock and add the soy sauce. Cover and cook for 4 hours on high or 6 ½ hours on low.

5. I love to eat this soup with little vegetable spring rolls – just dip them and eat.

● **Ham and Pork Soups**

Minestrone

This is a wonderfully easy version of the traditional Italian recipe.

Ingredients:
1 tbsp vegetable oil
200g streaky bacon or pancetta, chopped
1 clove garlic, chopped
2 sticks celery, chopped
2 carrots, chopped
1 red pepper, chopped
500ml chicken or ham stock
500ml passata
100g defrosted green beans
1 × 200g can cannellini beans, drained
½ tsp dried oregano
½ tsp dried thyme
½ tsp dried parsley
2 bay leaves
Salt and pepper

1. Heat the cooker on high and add the oil. Add the bacon or pancetta and the garlic. Cover and cook for 30 minutes.

2. Add the vegetables and stir well.

3. Heat the stock and passata together until just boiling and pour over the meat.

4. Add all the herbs and season to taste with salt and plenty of black pepper.

5. Cover and cook on high for 4 ½ hours or low for 7 hours.

6. Serve with lots of freshly grated parmesan or Grana Padano cheese.

Salami and Tomato

This is a rich tomato soup with the added deliciousness of salami.

Ingredients:
20g butter
1 small onion, chopped
1 potato, diced
1 carrot, chopped
1 × 400g can chopped tomatoes
4 tbsp tomato purée
125ml dry white wine
800ml stock or tomato juice
½–1 tsp dried basil or fresh basil to taste
1 × 200g can chickpeas
100g sliced salami

1. Heat the cooker on high and add the butter, onion, potato and carrot. Cover and cook for 20 minutes.

2. Put the tomatoes, purée, wine and stock or juice in a pan and heat to boiling. Pour into the cooker.

3. Stir in the basil and chickpeas. Cover and cook for 3 hours.

4. Chop the salami into small pieces and add to the cooker. Cover and cook for another 30 minutes.

Ham and Pork Soups

Fish and Seafood Soups

Seafood soup is best cooked on high as it cooks quite quickly and the flavour doesn't benefit from long cooking, as it does with meat.

Make a good flavoured stock using fish off-cuts, heads and bones from filleting. Simply boil them all together in sufficient water to cover, then simmer for 2 ½ hours. Strain and reduce by fast simmering if you wish. This will take about 20 minutes depending on the quantity.

You can use raw shellfish if you like, but I tend to use the ready-cooked type as it is quicker and tastes just as good. If you do use raw shellfish add 30–45 minutes to the cooking time just to be sure.

Seafood with Fennel

Ingredients:
2 tbsp sunflower or rapeseed oil
1 small onion, chopped
2 cloves garlic, chopped
4 baby fennel bulbs, chopped
200g fillet of trout, sea bream, cod or haddock, cut into bite-sized pieces
250g seafood cocktail, including prawns, mussels and squid, defrosted if frozen
Juice of 1 lemon
300ml passata
100ml dry white wine
Pinch saffron threads
600ml fish stock
2 tbsp freshly chopped parsley
1 tbsp capers
Salt and pepper to taste
Extra chopped parsley to serve

A luxurious, main meal dish, to spoil yourself. It takes just 2 hours to cook.

1. Heat the slow cooker on high and add the oil, onion, garlic and fennel.

2. Place the fish and seafood over the fennel. Squeeze the lemon juice over the fish and seafood.

3. Heat the passata, wine, saffron and stock in a pan until it boils.

4. Pour the stock mixture over the ingredients in the cooker and add the parsley and capers. Season with salt and pepper to taste.

5. Cover and cook for 2–2½ hours.

6. Add a little extra chopped parsley when serving.

● **Fish and Seafood Soups**

Salmon with Dill

The added touch of vermouth just makes this soup a little more special.

Ingredients:
1 tbsp sunflower oil
3 large spring onions, chopped
1 stick celery, chopped
80g mange tout, sliced
300g salmon fillets, cut into small pieces
2 rounded tbsp freshly chopped dill
1 litre fish stock, heated until hot
2 tbsp dry vermouth
Salt and pepper to taste
2 handfuls spinach
Fresh dill sprigs to serve

1. Heat the slow cooker on high and add the oil, spring onions, celery and mange tout.

2. Place the salmon over the top of the vegetables and spread the dill over the fish.

3. Combine the hot stock and vermouth and pour over the cooker ingredients. Season to taste.

4. Add the spinach and cover and cook for 3 hours on high.

5. Serve with some fresh dill sprigs.

Bouillabaisse

Ingredients:
3 tbsp olive oil
1 large onion, finely chopped
3 cloves garlic, chopped
2 tbsp tomato purée
5 ripe tomatoes, chopped
1 large potato, cubed
1 fillet each of salmon, haddock or
  pollack and whiting, each
  weighing about 100–120g, cut
  into small pieces
250g mixed shellfish: prawns,
  mussels, cockles and squid
A fresh bouquet garni: 2 large
  parsley stalks, 3 sprigs thyme and
  2 bay leaves, tied together with
  string
1 litre fish stock
200ml passata
Salt and black pepper
6 prawns, cooked and left in their
  shells

This is a real favourite of mine and is best made with real, homemade fish stock.

1. Heat the slow cooker on high and add the oil, onion, garlic, tomato purée, tomatoes and potato. Cover and cook for 30 minutes.

2. Add the fish to the cooker and the seafood on top. Place the bouquet garni on top.

3. Heat the stock and passata to boiling and pour over the fish mixture.

4. Cover and cook for 3–3 ½ hours. Remove the bouquet garni and stir before serving.

5. Add a whole prawn to each bowl of soup to serve.

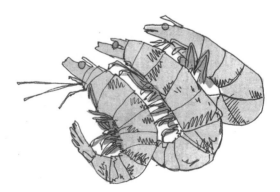

Mixed Fish and Vegetable

An economical dish that tastes like luxury.

1. Heat the slow cooker on high and add the oil or butter. Stir in the onion, celery, carrots and broccoli.

2. Cover and cook for 30 minutes.

3. Add the fish and stir in the stock and parsley. Season with salt and pepper to taste.

4. Cover and cook for 2½–3 hours on high. Add the peas and beans half way through the cooking time.

5. Add the parsley just before serving and serve with your favourite bread.

Ingredients:
2 tbsp vegetable oil or 15g butter
1 small onion, chopped
1 stick celery, chopped
2 carrots, chopped
6 florets broccoli, halved if large
300g mixed white fish (haddock, cod, coley, whiting or pollack), cut into small pieces
1.3 litres fish stock, heated until hot
1 tsp dried parsley
Salt and pepper to taste
100g fresh or frozen and defrosted peas
50g fresh or frozen and defrosted green beans, chopped into 2cm pieces
1–2 tbsp freshly chopped parsley

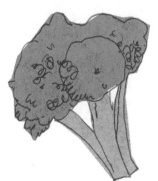

Paella-style

Ingredients:
2 tbsp olive oil
1 large onion, chopped
2 cloves garlic, chopped
1 red pepper, chopped
4 ripe tomatoes, chopped
1 tsp fresh thyme leaves
200g long-grain rice
1 litre fish or chicken stock, heated
    until hot
Pinch saffron threads
150g fillet of white fish, cut into
    small pieces
100g mussel meat
100g shelled prawns
100g small scallops
100g fresh or frozen and defrosted
    peas
Zest and juice of 1 lemon
120g chorizo, chopped
2 tbsp freshly chopped parsley

A favourite Mediterranean dish transformed into a soup.

1. Heat the slow cooker on high and add the oil, onion, garlic, pepper and tomatoes. Cover and cook for 20 minutes.

2. Add the thyme and rice.

3. Stir the saffron into the hot stock and pour into the cooker. Cover and cook for 1 hour.

4. Add the fish, shellfish, peas, lemon zest and juice and chorizo. Cover and cook for 1–2 hours.

5. Stir in the fresh parsley just before serving.

94

Smoked Haddock

This soup makes a really filling, tasty meal.

1. Heat the slow cooker on high and add the butter and onion. Cover and cook for 15 minutes.

2. Add all the other ingredients except for the cream. Cover and cook for 2½–3 hours on high.

3. Stir in the cream and cover and cook for 30 more minutes.

4. Serve with some extra fresh dill sprigs.

Ingredients:
15g butter
1 onion, finely chopped
400g smoked haddock, cut into small chunks
800ml fish or vegetable stock
120ml dry white wine
1 tbsp chopped dill
1 tsp black peppercorns, roughly crushed in a pestle and mortar
Salt to taste
150ml double cream
Extra fresh dill sprigs to serve

Fish with Lemon and Tarragon

Ingredients:
15g butter
400g white fish fillets, cut into small pieces
6 sprigs fresh tarragon
Juice of 2 lemons
1 lemon, cut into 6 slices with the pips removed
150ml dry white wine
1 litre fish stock
Salt and pepper to taste

A light, fresh-tasting soup, which makes an excellent starter dish.

1. Heat the slow cooker on high and add the butter and fish.

2. Place the tarragon on top of the fish and pour the lemon over all of the pieces of fish. Lay the slices of lemon on top.

3. Combine the wine and stock and heat to boiling, then pour into the cooker over the fish. Season with salt and pepper.

4. Cover and cook for 2–2 ½ hours.

5. Serve with some crusty bread.

• **Fish and Seafood Soups**

Mussels with Chilli and Garlic

This is another excellent starter course dish.

Ingredients:
20g butter
1 small onion or 3 shallots, very finely chopped
1 red chilli, chopped
4 cloves garlic, chopped
350g mussel meat
100ml dry white wine
700ml fish or vegetable stock
Salt and pepper to taste
1–2 tbsp freshly chopped parsley

1. Heat the slow cooker on high and add the butter, onion or shallots, chilli and garlic. Cover and cook for 15 minutes.

2. Add the mussels and stir into the other ingredients.

3. Heat the wine and stock to boiling and pour into the cooker. Season with salt and pepper to taste.

4. Cover and cook for 2 hours.

5. Serve topped with the extra parsley.

Crab

Ingredients:
20g butter
1 onion, finely chopped
1 stick celery, chopped
½ tsp cayenne pepper
1 clove garlic, chopped
700ml fish or vegetable stock, heated
   until hot
2 bay leaves
300g brown and white crabmeat
4 tbsp double cream

A real treat for crab lovers and it makes the meat go further.

1. Heat the slow cooker on high and place all the ingredients except for the crabmeat and cream in the cooker. Cover and cook for 1 hour or until it is simmering and bubbling.

2. Stir in the crabmeat and cover and cook for 45 minutes.

3. Stir in the cream and serve immediately with slices of melba toast.

Mediterranean Fish

If you wish to make this into a main course dish, double the amount of fish used.

Ingredients:
2 tbsp olive oil
2 cloves garlic, chopped
1 onion, finely chopped
1 green pepper, chopped
6 medium-sized mushrooms, sliced
12-15 black olives, chopped
600ml fish or vegetable stock
200ml dry white wine
1 × 400g can chopped tomatoes
1 tsp dried basil
½ tsp fennel seeds
250g white fish fillets
200g ready-to-use prawns
2 bay leaves
Salt and pepper

1. Heat the slow cooker on high and add the oil, garlic, onion and pepper. Cover and cook on high for 30 minutes.

2. Add the mushrooms and olives.

3. Heat the stock, wine and tomatoes together and pour into the cooker. Stir in the basil and fennel seeds.

4. Add the fish and prawns to the soup with the bay leaves and season to taste with salt and pepper.

5. Cover and cook for 2–2½ hours on high.

6. Serve with some ciabatta bread.

Winter-weight Soups

These soup recipes are designed to be winter warmers and I don't make any excuse for the use of butter and cream. Vegetables can be cut chunkier in these recipes.

If you need to soak dried vegetables and you forget to do it the night before, pour hot water over them and microwave for 10 minutes. Let them stand for at least 1 ½ hours before you need to use them. They will burst a bit but this won't affect the soup.

Thick Vegetable with Cheese Dumplings

Anything with dumplings appeals to me when I am hungry.

1. Heat the slow cooker on high and add the butter and all the fresh vegetables. Season with salt and pepper to taste. Cover and cook for 40 minutes on high.

2. Stir in the stock, peas, lentils and rice.

3. Cover and cook for 3 ½ hours on high or 6 hours on low.

4. Make the dumplings by sifting the flour, salt, mustard and cayenne together in a bowl. Stir in the suet and cheese. Mix in a little water 1 tsp at a time, until it becomes a soft, pliable dough.

5. Form into balls and drop into the soup 1 hour before the end of cooking time.

Ingredients:
15g butter
1 onion, chopped
3 carrots, sliced into discs
2 leeks, chopped
2 small turnips, diced
2 medium-sized potatoes
Salt and pepper
1.2 litres vegetable stock, heated until hot
150g defrosted frozen peas
80g red lentils
80g long-grain rice

For the dumplings:
100g self-raising flour
Pinch salt
1 tsp mustard powder
Pinch cayenne pepper
30g suet
40g Cheddar cheese, grated
Water to mix

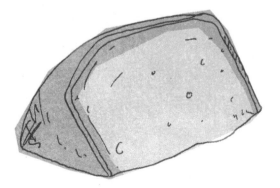

Cream of Vegetable

Ingredients:
1 onion, chopped
2 potatoes, diced
2 carrots, chopped
2 leeks, chopped
1 stick celery, chopped
1 red pepper, chopped
1 tsp dried thyme
500ml stock
600ml milk
25g butter
20g plain flour
100g defrosted and frozen, sliced
    green beans
Salt and pepper

One way of making this soup is to make a béchamel sauce with the milk and stock, but I prefer to put it all into the cooker and let it do its job. It just needs a jolly good stir all together first.

1. Heat the slow cooker on high and add the fresh vegetables and thyme. Cover and cook on high for 20 minutes.

2. Heat the stock and milk and when warm, add the butter and sprinkle in the flour. Stir well with a balloon whisk. Bring slowly to the boil then pour into the cooker with the vegetables.

3. Stir in the green beans and season with salt and pepper.

4. Cover and cook for 3 hours on high or 6 hours on low.

Thick Potato

This was a childhood favourite – my Dad used to make it for us this on foggy half-term holidays in October or November. But then it was made in a pan and took a lot of hard work and time to get a perfectly smooth soup. He would have loved a hand blender.

Ingredients:
15g butter
1 large onion, finely chopped
500g potatoes, diced fairly small
1 tsp dried thyme
800ml stock, heated until hot
200ml milk
Pinch nutmeg
Salt and pepper to taste (I always use white pepper for its strength in this recipe.)
100ml single cream

1. Heat the slow cooker on high and put all the ingredients in the cooker together, including the cream.

2. Stir well and cover and cook for 3 hours on high or 6 hours on low.

3. Blend the soup using a hand blender until it reaches the desired texture.

4. Add an extra knob of butter just before serving. Serve with hot, buttered toast. Ahh memories.

Mexican Hot Pot

Ingredients:
20g butter
1 large onion, chopped
1 potato, cubed
1 green pepper, chopped
300g minced beef
1 × 400g can chopped tomatoes
750ml stock
½ tsp chilli flakes
½ tsp cayenne pepper
1 × 400g can red kidney beans
1 × 200g can chickpeas
100g long-grain rice

A warming, chilli-based, thick soup.

1. Heat the slow cooker on high and add the butter, onion, potato and pepper. Cover and cook for 30 minutes.

2. Add the beef.

3. Combine the tomatoes, stock, chilli and cayenne in a pan and heat to boiling. Pour over the meat and vegetables.

4. Stir in the kidney beans, chickpeas and rice and stir well.

5. Cover and cook for 3 ½–4 hours on high or 7 hours on low.

6. Serve with some warm pitta bread and hummus, or garlic bread.

Pot-au-feu

A pot of fire – well not quite, but the horseradish does give it a kick.

Ingredients:
25g butter or 2 tbsp vegetable oil
2 onions, chopped
2 large carrots, sliced
1 smallish turnip, diced
1 stick celery, chopped
1 leek, chopped
450g braising steak, cubed
1 tsp mixed herbs
1.2 litres beef or vegetable stock, heated until hot
1 rounded tsp grated horseradish
4 large cabbage leaves, shredded
Salt and pepper to taste

1. Heat the slow cooker on high and add the butter or oil, onions, carrots, turnip, celery and leek. Cover and cook for 30 minutes.

2. Add the meat and herbs.

3. Stir the horseradish into the stock and pour into the cooker.

4. Stir in the cabbage leaves and season with salt and pepper.

5. Cover and cook on high for 4½–5 hours or on low for 7½–8 hours.

6. Serve with potato wedges.

Thick Beef and Vegetable

Ingredients:
2 tbsp oil or 15g butter
1 onion, finely chopped
2 carrots, sliced
1 stick celery, chopped
2 large potatoes, diced
6 frozen and defrosted cauliflower
   florets, halved
150g medium-sized mushrooms,
   thickly sliced
1 red pepper, chopped
2 tbsp tomato purée
450g beef shoulder steak, trimmed
   of excess fat and chopped
1.2 litre beef or vegetable stock,
   heated until hot
100g pearl barley
Salt and pepper

Another barley and beef soup that fills you up when
you're hungry.

1. Heat the cooker on high and add the oil or butter,
   vegetables and tomato purée. Cover and cook for
   20 minutes.

2. Add the meat, stock and barley, and season with
   salt and pepper to taste. Stir well and cover. Cook
   for 5 hours on high or 7½–8 hours on low.

3. Serve with some warm soda bread and butter.

Lamb Stewp

My children christened this when I served it to them. It is a simple but delicious dish in between a soup and a stew.

1. Heat the cooker on high and add the butter or oil and the vegetables and dried herbs. Cover and cook for 20 minutes.

2. Add the meat, stock, soaked pulses and beans, and bay leaves. Season to taste.

3. Cover and cook for 5–5 ½ hours on high or 7 ½–8 hours on low.

4. Serve with plenty of crusty bread.

Ingredients:
200g dried country soup mix (a mixture of lentil, beans and barley, specially mixed for making soups), soaked in cold water overnight
15g butter or 2 tbsp vegetable oil
1 onion, chopped
2 large potatoes, cubed
100g swede, cubed
2 large carrots, sliced into discs
1 tsp mixed herbs
450g lamb meat, cubed
1.3 litres lamb or vegetable stock, heated until hot
2 bay leaves
Salt and pepper

Cock-a-leekie

Ingredients:
15g butter
4–5 leeks, chopped
6 chicken thigh portions, trimmed of
    excess skin and fat
2 large potatoes, diced
1 litre chicken stock
200ml dry white wine
½ tsp dried sage
½ tsp dried thyme
100g long-grain rice
Salt and pepper to taste

A traditional flavour made easy in the slow cooker.

1. Heat the cooker on high and add the butter and leeks. Cover and cook for 20 minutes.

2. Place the thighs on the leeks and scatter the potatoes on top.

3. Heat the stock and wine until boiling and pour over the chicken and vegetables.

4. Add the herbs and rice and season to taste. Cover and cook for 4½ hours on high or 8 hours on low.

5. Remove the chicken and cut away all the meat from the bones. Place the meat back in the soup. Cover and cook for 40 more minutes on high.

6. Serve with any good bread.

Curried Fish

Not too spicy this one – if you want to hot it up, simply add medium or hot curry powder instead.

Ingredients:
15g butter
1 tbsp mild curry powder
1 onion, finely chopped
1 clove garlic, finely chopped
2 tbsp tomato purée
200g broccoli florets, halved
450g white fish, cut into chunks
Juice 1 lemon
1 litre fish stock, heated until hot
Salt and pepper to taste
100g shelled prawns
3 tbsp crème fraîche
Freshly chopped parsley to serve

1. Heat the cooker on high and add the butter, curry powder, onion, garlic and tomato purée.

2. Stir in the broccoli. Place the fish on top and squeeze the lemon juice over it. Stir all the ingredients so the fish is coated well in the flavours.

3. Pour over the stock and season to taste with salt and pepper. Cover and cook for 3½–4 hours on high or 6½ hours on low.

4. Stir in the prawns and crème fraîche and cover and cook on high for 30 more minutes.

5. Serve with some freshly chopped parsley.

New England Fish Chowder

Ingredients:

200g piece skinned belly pork, roasted in the oven for about 1 hour at 180°C/Gas Mark 4, then chopped into bite-sized pieces
15g butter
1 onion, chopped
250g potatoes, diced
400g cod, cut into chunks
50g button mushrooms, halved
800ml fish stock, heated until hot
100g sweetcorn, either fresh, canned, or frozen and defrosted
Salt and pepper to taste
100g white crabmeat
200ml single cream

A very hearty fish soup, combining pork belly, cod and crabmeat.

1. Heat the cooker on high and add the butter, onion and potatoes. Cover and cook for 30 minutes.

2. Add the fish, belly pork, mushrooms and stock and stir. If you are using fresh sweetcorn from the kernel, add it now also. Season to taste. Cover and cook for 3½–4 hours on high or 7½ hours on low.

3. Stir in the crabmeat, corn and cream and stir well. Cover and cook for 30 more minutes.

4. Serve with crispy croutons.

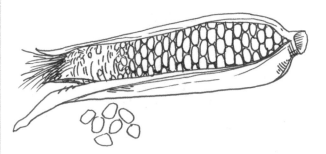

Index

Some other titles from How To Books

EVERYDAY FAMILY FAVOURITES
Over 300 delicious wholesome recipes that you can easily cook at home
DIANA PEACOCK

'The only book you'll need to feed a growing family, whatever you budget.'

If you want your children to remember chocolate cakes and apple pies and freshly baked bread; bubbling hot steak and kidney pies with buttered mash; wonderfully light and healthy pasta; sherry trifles at Christmas and treacle toffee on Bonfire night; and lots of other homemade family favourites, then this is the book for you.

With over 300 clear and concise recipes for delicious, nutritious and heart warming food, here is a book that revives old fashioned, traditional home cooking using good, fresh, local ingredients.

It will show you how to make inexpensive recipes that ensure you eat well every day of the week. From light snacks to hearty main courses and home baking, you will discover how a cleverly stocked store-cupboard and simple recipes make tasty family meals whatever your budget. You can also use it to make your own bacon, sausages, pickles, baked beans, butter, yoghurt, cream and cheese.

Put your heart back into your cooking with delicious recipes that turn out as they are meant to. This book will show you how to prepare all the decent food a family will ever need.

ISBN 978-1-908974-00-6

SWEET AND TREATS TO GIVE AWAY
DIANA PEACOCK AND REBECCA PEACOCK

This book will show you how to make all your favourite sweet treats at home – and then how to package them beautifully for giving away.

With a minimum of effort and equipment, you'll be able to wow your friends and make delicious, beautifully-packaged gifts that even the most difficult-to-buy-for-people will love!

With our detailed techniques and step-by-step illustrations, you'll be amazed how easy and enjoyable it is to make your own sweets. We'll even show you some ideas for creative presentation for all sorts of special occasions including weddings, birthdays and Christmas, so your goodies will look as good as they taste.

You'll find recipes for fudge, toffee, chocolates and traditional treats such as Turkish Delight, as well as other hamper favourites including liqueurs, sweet sauces and preserves.

Rebecca Peacock is a professional designer and a keen cook. She runs her own design business *Firecatcher* and is the author of *Make & Mend: a guide to recycling clothes and fabrics*. Diana Peacock has been making sweets and treats to give away for nearly 30 years. She is also the author of *Everyday Family Favourites, Good Home Baking, Good Home Preserves*, and co-author of *Grandma's Ways for Modern Days*.

ISBN 978-1-905862-86-3

THE HEALTHY LIFESTYLE DIET COOKBOOK
SARAH FLOWER

Tired of fad diets and yo-yo dieting? Do you want to lose weight and improve your health but still enjoy your food? Nutritionist Sarah Flower believes that by following the recipes in her book you can eat well, lose weight, feel better AND stay that way. Sarah's focus is on healthy eating and delicious food that all the family will enjoy. She also describes lifestyle changes that everyone can adopt to lay the foundations for healthy eating and to lose unwanted pounds if they need to. Sarah also includes superfoods, menu plans and some food swap suggestions.

ISBN 978-1-905862-74-0

MAKE YOUR OWN JELLIED PRESERVES
An easy guide to home and hedgerow jelly making
CAROLINE PAKENHAM

This book will show you how you can use the fruits and herbs you can grow in your garden, or the fruits that you can pick yourself from the hedgerows, to make into jars of delicious jelly preserves – quickly, easily, cheaply, and without fuss. It will enable even the true beginner to understand what to do, and feel confident and proud of their end product. The book includes full colour photos to help you recognise hedgerow fruits, plus numerous recipes for fruits that you can gather locally from spring to autumn or buy from further afield.

ISBN 978-1-905862-76-4

EAT WELL, SPEND LESS
The complete money-saving guide to everyday cooking
SARAH FLOWER

This invaluable book contains over 200 great family recipes for busy cooks who want to save time and money, but also deliver wholesome food for their families. It's also an essential housekeeper's guide for the 21st century. Nutritionist Sarah Flower shows you how to feed yourself and your family a healthy balanced diet without spending hours in the kitchen and a fortune in the supermarket.

ISBN 978-1-905862-83-2

EVERYDAY THAI COOKING
Easy, authentic recipes from Thailand to cook at home for friends and family
SIRIPAN AKVANICH

Everyday Thai Cooking brings you the secrets of cooking delicious Thai food straight from Thailand. Author Siripan Akvanich draws on her years of experience of cooking for her restaurant customers in Thailand to enable you to create authentic Thai dishes, ranging from curries and meat and fish dishes to wonderful Thai desserts. With clear instructions and insider tips, Siripan helps you bring these dishes – many of them traditional family recipes – to life and shows you how to make them *a-roi* (delicious)!

ISBN 978-1-905862-85-6

EVERYDAY COOKING FOR ONE
Imaginative, delicious and healthy recipes that make cooking for one fun
WENDY HOBSON

Here is a collection of simple, tasty meals – specially designed for one – that can help you enjoy your everyday eating. Starting with sensible tips for shopping and for stocking your food cupboard, you'll find recipes for everything from snacks to delicious fish; and meat and vegetable main courses that keep an eye on a healthy dietary balance – and a healthy bank balance. And there's a unique feature, too. Some recipes just don't work in small quantities, and that could include some of your favourites. So we've included some of those recipes – like casseroles, roasts and cakes – and show you how to create four different meals from one single cooking session.

ISBN 978-1-905862-94-8

How To Books are available through all good high street and on-line bookshops, or you can order direct from us through Grantham Book Services.

Tel: +44 (0)1476 541080
Fax: +44 (0)1476 541061
Email: orders@gbs.tbs-ltd.co.uk

Or via our website

www.howtobooks.co.uk

To order via any of these methods please quote the title(s) of the book(s) and your credit card number together with its expiry date.

For further information about our books and catalogue, please contact:

How To Books
Spring Hill House
Spring Hill Road
Begbroke
Oxford
OX5 1RX

Visit our web site at

www.howtobooks.co.uk

Or you can contact us by email at info@howtobooks.co.uk

Like our Facebook page How To Books & Spring Hill

Follow us on Twitter @Howtobooksltd

Read our books online www.howto.co.uk